FRACTURED

FRACTURED

My Journey Back from Death
and the Lessons
I Learned Along the Way

Elizabeth Antonucci

easp publications

Cover design by Melissa Tenpas.
Cover image: rost9/stock.adobe.com.
Interior design by
Meadowlark Publishing Services.
Author photo by Ian McLaren, ianmclaren. photography. All other photos are the author's.
ISBN 978-0-9989104-0-6
Published by easp publications
www.elizabethantonucci.com.

Manufactured in the United States of America.
Published 2017.

dedicated to sam wasson
and my family

Contents

CONTENTS

A Letter
to the Reader

I don't have many true fears in life. People who know me know I'm terrified of bridges and those grated things in the sidewalk. Definitely irrational, but I don't have any plans to conquer those fears any time soon—I am 100 percent okay with being scared of these things for the rest of my life. But my biggest fear, the one that I am in the process of overcoming, is my fear of the unknown. It has held me back from a lot in my life. In a weird way, while it sometimes paralyzes me and creates a block, it is also my biggest motivator and source of excitement. Signing up for a class, writing this book, deciding to pursue a different career, waking up every day ... all of these terrify and excite me because of the unknown. While some cause me less anxiety than others, the common denominator is fear. My dad has always told me, "Anything worth losing is worth chasing after. If you aren't scared of it, maybe it really isn't worth doing." Just think about that ... isn't that so true? Oh, how

I wish I would have learned how right my parents were at an earlier age.

The first time this hit me in my core was in 2011, shortly after I founded my theater production company, Step Up Productions (now called Step Up Chicago Playwrights). I had spent quite some time trying to figure out what our first show was going to be. Not wanting to rush into it, I read countless scripts, many of which I loved, but none really felt like the right one to have as our debut. But then, in the fall of 2011, I read *The Sweetest Swing in Baseball* by Rebecca Gillman and I knew, from five pages in, that this was the one.

I immediately took the script to my dad and asked him to read it. He loved it and said we had a hit on our hands. Then I took it to my mentor, Audrey Francis, whom I asked to direct. When I applied for rights and was granted permission to produce the show, it finally became real. I vividly remember sitting on my parents' living room couch and my dad asking me, "How do you feel?" My response was, "Terrified." He said, "Good— that means it will all be worth it."

This was a turning point for me. I'd never really thought about fear in that way. I'd always viewed it as a negative, as something that will hold you back from doing what you want and accomplishing all you can. From that day on I learned that fear can be your biggest motivator. The fear of making our Chicago debut was what drove me to work as hard and as smart as I could to make it a success.

For the longest time, the fear of writing this book

kept me from doing it. I first conceived the idea for it back in 2008. Since then it has taken many forms but always with the same intention—to help others. Yet it actually started as therapy for me. After a serious car accident that took my friend's life and almost took mine, I started writing down my memories as a way to process what I was going through and what had happened. I originally thought I wanted to write a one-woman show based on different stories from my recovery process, but that didn't get very far. Something always kept me from writing, from releasing the information in my brain to the page. It was a block created mostly by fear, but I now know the one-woman show wasn't the project I needed to write—this book was. Once I knew the story I wanted to tell, and clearly defined the message I wanted to share, it was like the floodgates opened. But as soon as I decided I needed to tell my truth, fear came rushing in. I had ideas, stories, and experiences I wanted to share, but every time I sat down to write, nothing came out.

Things started to shift for me in the summer of 2015 when I decided it was time to stop running from the fear and instead *lean into it*. I met with a friend from high school, Dana Marie (an amazing singer-songwriter now living in Nashville), who gave me the name of a literary company, KN Literary Arts. I was so excited after my initial phone call with them that I called my mom and said, "This is it. I know I can have this book complete in the next two months." Ha! I was a little overconfident. What followed were a few very trying months of not getting as far as I thought I would, numerous back-and-forth phone calls with my writing coach, Rebecca, and lots of time spent staring at a blank page. I was ready to give up. But something in me told me to keep at it. So early in 2016 I made a decision to write every single day for an hour a day and not judge myself for what I had written, what I had (or hadn't) accomplished. I would just sit down at my computer for an hour, look at the outline I had created, and write whatever inspiration came. I decided it was time to stop running from the fear of this huge unknown adventure and start diving into it head first.

I had made this promise to myself before. I told myself to just sit down for sixty minutes a day and write, but I got frustrated staring at the blank page. I let the fear of certain points in my outline keep me from developing the story. My fear of being vulnerable and really opening up about an experience kept me from wanting to delve into it. Finally, though, I decided it was time for me to make the conscious choice to develop my ideas and really share the most vulnerable and scary parts of myself with you. I do not know what will happen to this book or how it will be received. I do not know what people will think of me before, during, or after reading it. But I do know that if I help one person, share my truth, and let people know they are not alone, I will have done my job.

When I was thinking about what I wanted this book to be, I always said, "If I could go back and tell my high school self everything I know now, life would be so much easier." That's what I want from this book. I want to help those who have gone through, or are going through, something scary or difficult to realize that they are not alone. Life is terrifying, life is exhilarating, and life is challenging all at the same time, and it is helpful to know someone else has gone through the same craziness. Someone else has done it and has made it out alive—in my case, literally made it out alive. The unknown can keep you small. It can keep you quiet and make you into someone you're not, preventing you from embracing who you are truly meant to be.

When I broke down on my thirtieth birthday, my therapist and my mom both kept telling me, "You are not being as big as you know you can be." I had no idea what they were talking about. They kept saying, "You have so much to share and you are not doing that, you have no clue what your true potential is. Why are you keeping yourself from your *bigness?*" After my frustration settled and my tears dried, I realized it was because of my old friend *fear*. Once again, I had let fear of the unknown keep me on the sidelines.

I can't say that every day is a great day, or that I'm always able to prevent fear from getting in my way, but I can say that now, whenever I start to feel like I can't do something because I don't know what the result will be, I try to reframe my thinking to focus on the positive. "When I finish this (fill in the blank), imagine what can happen." It is a little way for me to keep my fear under control. I spend some time visualizing the outcome. What that success looks like to me. How I will feel and what I will wear. I try to recognize the types of scents I might smell and to relish in them. This helps me feel more in control.

For you, the reader, I hope this book helps you find love, laughter, power, and relief. I hope you are able to recognize yourself in some of my stories and know that there is a light at the end of whatever tunnel you are traveling through. I hope my words resonate, and you are able to take what I have learned and apply it to your life.

While all these stories and events are true, some of the names have been changed to protect privacy.

PART ONE

The Accident

1

THE DETAILS

It was the fall semester of my senior year at Loyola Marymount University in Los Angeles, California. I was a theater major, working at a wonderful production company, Mandalay Entertainment. I was enjoying life and had just been cast in the play *The Laramie Project*. Following in the footsteps of the Tectonic Theater Project, the original group that wrote the play, we drove to Laramie, Wyoming, to conduct research. We spoke with people who had known Matthew Shepard and interviewed members of the community. Five of us had to return to LMU earlier than the rest of the cast because we were going into tech week for another play, *The Rocky Horror Picture Show*. Steve, David, Jack, Tony, and I left Monday night.

Early Tuesday morning, October 23, 2007, around 3:00 a.m., we were driving through Utah near a town called Fillmore. Tony was at the wheel, Jack was sleeping in the right front seat, Steve and I were sleeping in the backseat, and David was sleeping behind us in the far back of the Infiniti SUV. Tony set the car on cruise control at 90 mph and accidently nodded off. When he woke up, he overcorrected his driving; the car flipped and rolled seven times. David and I were ejected through the sunroof, and I landed fifty feet (some reports say fifty yards) from the car. Steve, who was shaken up but conscious, got out of the SUV, ran up the exit ramp, crossed the highway, found a pay phone, and called the police for help. Then he went back to the car, pulled Tony and Steve out, and laid them on the ground.

The town we were near was so small that there was only one police officer, and the person who answered Steve's call had to reach him at his home. He then had to call the highway patrol and, since Steve wasn't familiar with the area, it took them over an hour to find us. Then the highway patrol had to contact the emergency ambulance unit and they had to come get us. All told, we lay there for at least an hour, maybe two.

We were taken to a very small regional hospital in Fillmore where our injuries could be assessed. The doctors determined that David's injuries and my own were too severe to treat there (I had a broken neck, nose, shoulder, shoulder blade, arm, and ankle), and we needed to be transferred to another hospital more than a hundred miles away. David was airlifted out first. I was airlifted next, and Jack followed by ambulance to Utah Valley Regional Medical Center in Provo. During this time, I was unconscious except for probably ten seconds when I woke up long enough to whisper my dad's cell phone number to a nurse.

I can't even imagine the terror my parents felt that night. It haunts me every time I think about it. I don't remember anything, but from what I was told, my dad answered the call. I think the words he heard were "Your daughter has been in an accident—we don't think she is going to make it. You better come out here." He then called my mom, who was on her way to work out. They got the last two seats on a flight to Utah. When they arrived at the hospital they were told, "Your daughter is going to live, but she may not walk or talk again."

From what my parents have told me, the next three weeks were a nightmare. I have a vague memory of them walking through the door of my hospital room. I was going in and out of consciousness and remember them having to explain to me what had happened every time I came to. Everything was such a blur and moving so quickly. Doctors were in and out of my room, people were poking and prodding me in different places, and I was submitted to test after test. My parents knew David had passed away, but they didn't tell me for about a week because my condition was so critical. And I was already agitated enough.

The doctors advised my parents that I needed a spinal fusion and neck surgery. These were risky procedures so my dad called a family friend, a surgeon who gave my parents the name of a doctor in Salt Lake City, the head of neurology. My dad called him and explained the situation, and I was transferred by ambulance to Salt Lake City's University of Utah Medical Center. It was there that I would have my surgery and spend the rest of my hospitalization. My dad eventually had to go back home—my younger brother was just a freshman in high school—so my aunt flew out to stay with my mom by my side.

2

FROM UTAH TO CHICAGO

I spent about a month in hospitals, with the doctors monitoring my recovery from my shoulder and arm fracture and the fusion of the C6 and C7 vertebrae. They were trying to anticipate and address any further complications, and put a plan into action for when I returned home. The most pressing concern was vertigo, the result of my brain injury—I was dizzy whenever I moved. I wasn't yet able to sleep through the night and my pain wasn't completely under control. I would need to undergo extensive rehabilitation once I was back in Chicago.

In November 2007, I was finally released. I was excited and scared. I didn't know how I was going to be able to make it to the airport and onto a plane—I could barely make it around the nurses' station with help. I had no clothes with me, so my mom went out and bought me something I could wear for the trip home. It took some time to get me dressed and into a wheelchair. I was terrified to get back into a car. My mom drove extremely slowly and carefully, but even so I was nauseous and extremely anxious. I believe the airport was only about thirty minutes away, but it felt like a two-hour trip. When we finally arrived, I waited for someone to bring a wheelchair to the car.

Next we had to battle our way through the security line. They wouldn't let me go through in a wheelchair so my mom and my aunt had to help me through a special portion of the line. Security had to swab my neck brace, which I couldn't take off without a huge hassle. They also had to swab my arm, which was in a sling, as well as my wheelchair. I finally got the okay to continue, and we headed to the gate. I was really nauseous and wanted to take pills for that, but couldn't handle them on an empty stomach. My mom got me something to eat, but I couldn't really lift my arms or hold a fork, so she had to feed me. This scared me. How was I ever going to get better? Would I be able to have a normal life again? Everyone was staring.

I took my pills, and we were the first ones to board the plane. Thank goodness my mom had gotten us seats in the first row—I don't think I could have walked much farther.

The flight felt like it lasted a lifetime; I thought I would never get off that plane. I was particularly nervous about the takeoff and landing because I know those have the most impact on your body. Thankfully, they weren't that bad and I had my mom and aunt on either side of me, which was a huge comfort.

In Chicago we were the first ones to get off the plane, and there was someone waiting with a wheelchair. We made our way down to the baggage claim, where my aunt and my mom collected their bags. It was freezing in Chicago! I was so cold, and nervous about the ride back to my house. Chicago is not known for the best drivers in the world, and getting in the car was the last thing I wanted to do.

My mom and my aunt helped me in and explained to the driver that I was really scared—they didn't care how long it took to get home, but he needed to go slowly. He did, and thankfully I made it without any major problems. Yes, I was dizzy and nauseous but, other than that, I was okay.

We pulled into the driveway and I was thrilled to be done with travel. My mom, my aunt, and I squeezed through the door of our house and my whole family was home: my dad, my older sister, Cristina, my younger sister, Jenna, who had flown home from college, and my brother, Joe. My aunt and my mom helped me into our living room and brought me a chair. I was so happy to be there, but I felt like someone had sucked the life out of me. I didn't respond to anyone. My parents tell me I just had a "void" look on my face. I lasted about two minutes before I got so tired that I needed to go to bed.

My cousins, who own a medical supply company, gave my family a hospital bed so I could sleep in my dad's office on the first floor of the house—there was no way I was going to be able to make it up the stairs. It took a long time to get me out of my clothes and into some sort of pajamas. For five months after the surgery, I would have to wear a large cervical collar brace. Whenever I got into bed, I couldn't lie back because of the neck brace and vertigo, so I was almost always sitting up. At this point, I wasn't talking much either. I had a very limited vocabulary, and it was hard for me to retrieve words and formulate sentences.

Those first couple of nights my dad slept in the room with me. There wasn't much sleep. I was up every hour or so with terrible night sweats—I would wake up dripping. I also suffered from night terrors, flashbacks of the accident or of me lying on the side of the road. I heard cars screeching or crashing outside the window. This continued for the first couple of months I was home. Actually, to this day, I am not able to sleep with my window open because, inevitably, I will wake up in the middle of the night hearing imaginary cars colliding.

Within the first few weeks of being home, I got the flu, a bladder infection, and horribly high fevers. I was on round-the-clock medication and pain pills. I had no appetite, and I don't think I smiled once. I didn't do anything except sit in bed and take naps.

My aunt visited almost every day, and Cristina came over whenever she wasn't in school. Veronica, who had entered our lives when I was five in order to help my mom with our home and to raise four kids, and who had become part of the family, was also often by my side.

They sat with me whenever my mom was in the other room. I never wanted to be alone—that's when things got scary. I heard things, the room spun, and flashes of the accident flooded my brain.

As soon as I returned home, friends and family wanted to come over right away. Some of my parents' friends stopped by to say hi, but due to my energy level (or lack thereof), I wasn't really able to spend time with anyone. I can't remember much from those early months (a lot of these stories are pieced together from what my family has told me), but I know everybody was very supportive and loving, and I am so appreciative of that!

3

Struggle to See the Light

Life isn't about waiting for the storm to pass ... it's about learning to dance in the rain.
—*Vivian Greene*

I wasn't even home a week when my mom and my therapist and family friend, Wini, walked into the room. I had been seeing Wini for therapy since I was about fourteen years old.

My mom told me I'd be starting rehab later that week. I was immediately overcome with fear and broke down sobbing. How was I going to get through rehab? I argued that I wasn't ready. I couldn't get dressed by myself, I couldn't go to the bathroom by myself, and I couldn't have a conversation for more than two minutes without passing out from exhaustion. All I wanted to do was sleep. My mind was flooded with questions and fear of the unknown. What kinds of people were going to be there? Would they be my age? Would they all be older? Were the therapists going to be nice? Would they know how slowly I was going to have to take things? And the biggest question of all, and the one that scared me the most: was I going to have to leave my mom? I didn't want to leave her side for more than thirty seconds. I couldn't do anything without her; I depended on her for everything.

Clearly, I lost the argument about starting rehab. Three days a week I went to the Rehabilitation Institute of Chicago (RIC), and the other two days I went downtown to Rush University Medical Center to see my neck surgeon and an orthopedic doctor for my shoulder.

On a typical day I woke up between 6 and 7 a.m. (depending on whether I had to shower in the morning), got dressed, had something for breakfast, and was at the RIC by 8:30 a.m. I went to rehab from 8:30 to 11:30, and then my mom took me home and I slept. Sometimes I napped until dinnertime or until my mom woke me up. She didn't let me slumber too long for fear that I wouldn't be able to sleep through the night.

She also had to make sure I took walks around our house to prevent bedsores and keep my muscles from atrophying. At first I could only walk down the hallway and back. In time, I made it all the way around the kitchen and into the living room. My mom always put on music, usually Elvis (he's our favorite), and she danced and sang along while trying to get me to laugh and have a little bit of fun. But all I ever wanted to do was get back in bed and sleep. Eventually, as I started to get my strength back, I sometimes sang or laughed while walking with my parents or Cristina. My mom tried her hardest to schedule my doctor appointments for days when I didn't have rehab, but occasionally I had to do both. On those days I came home and crashed.

For the first couple of weeks of rehab, I was completely out of it. I had that same "blank" and "void" look—my mom calls it "the trauma look"—as I did when I first came home. At rehab there were mostly older people: stroke victims, car accident victims, MS patients, motorcycle accident victims, among others. There was really only one other person who was close to my age. She was about thirteen years old; a gymnastics accident had left her with limited limb function.

The old men did anything and everything they could to get me to smile, but I wasn't having it—I was completely checked out and not myself. I would get there, my mom would sit me down in a chair, and I would wait for one of my three therapists to come and get me. I had physical, occupational, and speech therapists. After my first hour-long session I would go back to the waiting area and wait for my next therapist to come get me. This repeated until all three of my sessions were complete. For the first couple of months or so I made sure my mom came with me to all of my therapy. I had such bad separation anxiety and was so vulnerable that I got extremely panicky and broke down if she left or I couldn't see her.

As I started to warm up to the people at rehab, I

began to make friends with the other patients there. The old men saved chairs for me so I could sit beside them. One man in particular, a stroke victim named Arnie, wouldn't leave for his therapy sessions until I arrived. I eventually started to look forward to talking with him and hearing what he had done the night before. One thing I remember vividly is that every day at 10:30 a.m., Arnie ate a banana. He was in a wheelchair and always pushed it as close to mine as he could. He had the best stories and one of the most positive outlooks. I remember being so amazed that he could laugh as much as he did.

As time went on, I slowly learned how to walk on my own and regained my balance. I discovered how to swallow again in a way that decreased the risk of choking, and I did a lot of word retrieval exercises to improve my brain function and recover the vocabulary I had lost.

One day my doctors and therapists told me that instead of having my occupational therapy session, I was going to see the psychologist. I broke down in tears. My family knew I was depressed, but I was in denial. Plus, I already had Wini, and I didn't want to talk to anybody new.

For the first few sessions, I asked my mom to come in with me. I didn't want to be left alone for a whole hour with someone I didn't know. The therapist basically helped me understand that it was totally normal for me to be depressed. Before the accident, I had been very independent. I was living in California, finishing school in a theater program I adored, and really enjoying my time working at the production company, surrounded by an industry that I loved. And now I couldn't do anything and was dependent on everybody.

The therapist explained to me that feeling ashamed that I had lived and David hadn't was normal. "You have survivor's guilt," I remember her saying. But why would I feel guilty for being alive? It was a subconscious and natural reaction for anyone who had gone through something like I had. My mom kept telling me that things would return to normal and everything was going to be okay, but at that point, I wasn't so sure I believed her.

The doctors, therapists, and other patients at RIC played a major role in my recovery. Every single one of them really took an interest in me, as they do in all their patients—their top priority was to help us get better. They took time to get to know me and learn my likes, dislikes, hobbies, interests, and background. They treated my mind, body, and spirit, which is extremely important after any kind of traumatic accident, and aided in all aspects of my recovery.

4

Laughing Through the Pain

Sometimes, in order to make it through tough moments, you have to find things to laugh about. Here are a few of my favorite stories that my family still likes to tell. If you are going through something difficult, just remember there is humor in every situation, even the darkest, scariest ones. Try to surround yourself with people who can help you find the funny and who can make you smile. Even if it's just for a short moment, it makes all the difference.

No, Dad, I Have to Go!
Whenever I tell this story, people laugh. Although I don't have much memory of it, my parents repeated it to me all the time whenever I felt like I wanted to give up.

When my parents first arrived at the hospital, I

was going in and out of consciousness—every time I woke up, my mom or dad had to explain to me what had happened and why I was lying in a hospital bed. Over and over, my dad told me that I'd been in a car accident. I had different responses each time: shock, tears, disbelief.

One time, after he explained to me what had happened, I told him I had to go. He said I couldn't leave and asked why I was in such a hurry. Trying to formulate sentences, I frantically explained as well as I could that I had a meeting with James Gandolfini's agent and a casting director from Warner Brothers Studios (which was true; it had been set up for me before I took my trip out to Wyoming). He carefully told me that I wasn't going to be able to make it to the meeting and that I would have to reschedule. Needless to say, I was not happy at all. As an aspiring actor at the time, I knew this was a big opportunity. I told my dad to get on the phone, call my friend in LA, have him pick up my headshots, and make sure they got to the meeting. He did, and my headshots made it to the meeting, even though I did not.

Paging Dr. McDreamy

One of the few things I clearly remember from my hospital stay is all of my hot doctors. They were all so cute! I thought I was at Seattle Grace Hospital in an episode of *Grey's Anatomy*. Every doctor who came into my room was cuter than the one before. It made all the exams, tests, and needles a little bit easier to handle.

Toward the end of my stay, one of the hunky doctors arrived to take the stitches out of my chin. As soon as he came in, I shot a look at my mom—she knew I was thinking about how cute he was. She started to laugh a little and I wondered what she knew that I didn't. When he was done removing my stitches he rubbed my shoulder and told me I had been one of his favorite patients ... I about died. When he left, my mom and I chatted about how attractive he was and she couldn't hold it in anymore—she started laughing. She then filled me in: he had been the one who had to do my vaginal exam when I was first admitted in order to make sure none of my bones or muscles had been damaged ... great!

Halloween

It was three days after my C6-C7 fusion—I was still very out of it and on a lot of heavy drugs. My mom and aunt had been traveling back and forth between the hospital and the hotel where they were staying. They were usually there when I woke up, but this morning they hadn't yet arrived. I remember watching the nurses and doctors walk by my room and noticing something weird—people were dressed up. I couldn't understand what was going on; why did everyone have costumes on? As soon as my mom walked in, I explained to her that I was hallucinating. "We should have the doctors check my meds because there is something wrong." She started laughing and told me that it was Halloween—it was completely normal for people to dress up.

Why?

This is one of my sister Cristina's favorite stories. Coming home from the hospital, I was still very much out of it and my thought process was not very clear. I was lying in my hospital bed with my mom and sister in the room and we were talking about the accident. I asked them why, if I was ejected out of the sunroof, the rest of the people in the car didn't just pull me back in? Both my mom and my sister started chuckling. I was dead serious; I was even crying at this point. I didn't understand why they hadn't just pulled me back into the car. They both must have been laughing for a good two minutes before they stopped and noticed that I was serious and crying. They then had to sweetly explain to me that the car was going so fast and everybody else in the car was scared and didn't know what was going on. I now realize that my question was pretty funny, but at the time, I was serious.

If You Can Cure Cancer …
You Can Help Me Pee!

When I was in the hospital I couldn't get in and out of bed to make it to the bathroom, so I had to have a catheter. Toward the end of my stay it came time to take it out. The catheter wasn't painful, and up until this point, it wasn't something I even knew I had. The thought of it really creeped me out, though, so I was thrilled when it came time to remove it … I should've known better. I had no clue about a major side effect of taking one out: I had to relearn how to pee.

I figured, no big deal, when I had to "go," I would just "go." Ha, right! Think again. One day I had to pee so badly and I couldn't. While the catheter was in place, the muscles in my bladder didn't have to work, so they weakened and, as the doctors phrased it, "got lazy." When it came time for me to "go" on my own, I simply couldn't. My bladder would get so full that it was extremely painful. I'd sit on the toilet and try so hard to pee, but I'd end up in tears. My mom and dad were laughing at the situation (I guess if I was in their shoes I would have been laughing too). Looking back now, it *was* pretty funny.

It got to the point where it was so bad, I made my dad call Jon Sweeney, the healer that I work with, to see if he could get me to pee. If you saw what this looked like, you would be dying laughing. I was on the toilet, my mom was holding me there (I had no balance), and my dad was on the phone in the hospital room with Jon. I was screaming at Jon from the bathroom, "You can put cancer into remission, Jon, you should be able to make me pee!"

Ultimately I couldn't pee and the doctors had to put the catheter back in. I hoped that the next time I had to pee it would be easier.

Don't Choke

My sister Cristina is a hypochondriac; she thinks she has every disease imaginable. She has a PsyD in clinical psychology and has spent countless hours research-ing, studying, and reading about every possible disease, neurosis, and condition, which only makes her situation worse—she thinks she might have everything she studies in her psych books. Cristina came up to the 'burbs whenever she had a chance to, and I loved being able to spend time with her. It made me feel less damaged. She brought me my favorite snacks and goodies. I couldn't eat large portions and I had difficulty swallowing, so my food always had to be cut into bite-size pieces, the way you would cut up food for an infant.

For someone who is neurotic, this was quite a predicament. Cristina took it one step further and tried to cut the food even smaller. Every time she did this I made fun of her, which made me laugh, which only made her fear of my choking greater. I never actually choked, but maybe I pretended to once or twice in order to mess with her.

Showers

Taking a shower was always a big ordeal for me; I couldn't walk by myself or hold my head up without my neck brace, and I only had one arm that worked. Whenever I needed a shower I had to enlist the help of my mom and another person—either my Auntie Jo, my sister Cristina, or Veronica. Showers went like this:

> My mom/aunt/Cristina/Veronica helped me into my parents' bathroom and sat me on the edge of the bathtub.
>
> One of them assisted me in taking off my

clothes (talk about learning to be comfortable with being uncomfortable!).

I was helped into the shower and situated on the medical chair in there.

After I was sitting and stable, my aunt or my mom took off my neck brace and held my head while someone else held my body and the shower hose.

Someone washed my body.

When it came time to wash my hair, I held a towel over my face so water and soap wouldn't get in my eyes, my aunt held my neck, and my mom washed my hair.

I was then rinsed off and helped out of the shower.

I lay on my parents' bed, the pillows propping up my head, while the pads in my neck brace were changed. This part was always a challenge. All of the pads looked the same, and it was hard to remember which went where.

To put the neck brace back on, one person needed to push the bed down so there was a gap between my neck and the pillow large enough to slide the back of the neck brace through. They then placed the front of the neck brace on and attach the two pieces together.

Finally I was able to get dressed. They helped me put on my clothes, including compression socks to keep my legs from getting blood clots, a second pair of socks with rubber on the bottom so I wouldn't slip on our hardwood floors, and two big tank tops that I pulled up from my legs. At long last I was able to put on my pants.

I then moved to a chair so they could dry my hair.

Although I always felt better after the ordeal was over because I was clean, I was often exhausted because it took so long: all told, usually about an hour to an hour and a half. I showered about two to three times a week, but only washed my hair once.

Let me be the first to tell you: you lose all sense of modesty and self-consciousness when you have to go through something like this. I was completely naked for a good forty-five minutes while three other people washed me and chatted as if everything was normal. The first time I was super uncomfortable, but after about three minutes that went away. Family. They are the greatest at making uncomfortable situations the best. They laughed with me, laughed at the situation we were in, and purposely did funny things to try to make me laugh and make everything a little more bearable.

I used to dread those showers (I am sure my family did too). But after the first couple of times, they became something I looked forward to. They created a bond between Cristina, my Auntie Jo, Veronica, my mom, and me, something we will always remember. These four women are my heroes and my angels. If you can't be comfortable and your true self around your family, who can you be that way with? Yes, I had no other choice, but the choice I did have was whether to make the most of it. My aunt would call the house and ask when our next "date" was. My dad would always say, "Oh boy, it's a big day ... shower day." Little excitements like this made these abnormal things more doable, more normal. Our lives had all been turned upside down, but instead of letting that play out in a negative way, my family really made the most of everything.

5

BEING HOME

Being at home was weird for me. I had some friends around, but most of them were still at school finishing up their senior year. I really do have the best family and friends in the whole world. They did everything and anything they could to get me to smile on a day-to-day basis. Sometimes they were more successful than others, but they never stopped trying.

For the first couple of months, I was only able to see one or two people a day, and I could really only talk to them for about two to five minutes at a stretch. My sister came over a lot and watched funny movies with me. Our films of choice were *Knocked Up* and *Borat*. These kept us laughing. We rarely talked about the accident; we just hung out together.

Sometimes my friends came over after rehab and had lunch. These simple, everyday things meant the world to me. It was so important for me to be surrounded by friends, family, and people who knew me and could support me.

There were days when I made plans for people to come over at a certain time but my mom or dad had to tell them to leave because I was sleeping or so exhausted and depressed that I couldn't talk to anyone. They left with no questions asked and came back another day. They weren't mad or annoyed that they had traveled all that way only to have to immediately turn around. I can't thank them enough, those friends and family who understood what I was going through and were there for me, making my fight for full recovery a little easier.

Oftentimes it was the little things that made the biggest difference. So many people sent me cards. My mom's friend Laura sent me one every week, sometimes twice a week! It made me feel so good and I always looked forward to getting the mail. My mom and dad hung the cards on the wall in my room, adding more each day. I must have gotten over three hundred or so—I still have them all saved. When my parents moved and we were packing up all of our things, I found them again. Reading through all the well wishes and seeing the names of so many different people who were rooting for me was incredible. I attribute all of my success and recovery to their support. They kept me going. I had something to fight for.

▲　▼　▲

My best friend, Corey, was at school in Virginia, so the first time I was able to see him was over Thanksgiving break. He and his then girlfriend, Becky (now his wife), were driving back home, which was about a thirteen-hour drive. They were driving at night, through a snowstorm, and the last place I wanted them to be was on the road. The entire time I called him about every thirty minutes or so to make sure he and Becky were okay. I was a nervous wreck! I had fallen asleep early (I probably exhausted myself from all the worrying), so they both came over the next day. It was so great to see them. We chatted about school and then we started talking about the accident. Corey told me that he'd found out in a roundabout way, through an ex-boyfriend of mine who, at that point, I hadn't spoken to in almost six months. At first Corey didn't really think it was true. He immediately called my dad, who explained to him what had happened, where we were, and what was going on. He told me that throughout the call he could hear me in the background asking to talk to him. I don't remember any of this, but he said we spoke. He said he was so relieved when he knew that I was going to be okay and that the rumors flying around on Facebook and through secondhand sources weren't true.

I wanted him and Becky to stay so we could catch up, but about four minutes into the conversation my eyes started to close. My mom and dad had to ask them to leave—I was losing the fight to stay awake. Corey would have come over seven days a week if I'd asked him to. If we didn't speak on the phone every day, we talked via text message. He was a really big part of my recovery and, throughout this process, he has been one of my most influential friends in helping me get back to my "normal" life.

▲　▼　▲

As I got stronger, my mom and I felt comfortable about her leaving my side for a couple of hours so she could run errands; however, she hired "babysitters" for me whenever she went out. I was completely mortified by this. She would tell me, "They aren't here to babysit you—they're just here to hang out." Right. I knew they were coming over to babysit me. Why else would my mom's friends come over to "hang out" when she wasn't going to be there? She was never away too long because even though my separation anxiety had gotten better, it was still not completely gone. She was always available via phone and text so I always knew where she was.

Even though I was embarrassed and didn't think I needed a babysitter (which I clearly did because I was still very unstable on my own), I am so thankful to the people who came and sat with me. It was kind of them to do so, and I very much appreciate it now. I want to thank everyone who came to "hang out." I want to thank "the birthday club" for sending cards, flowers, meals, gifts, and everything else. It meant the world to my family and me to have that type of support. They helped keep my spirits up and kept me fighting each and every day, even when I didn't want to fight anymore.

6

Spiritual Medium— Julie Walker

I have grown up in a family that values all types of healing—physical, mental, emotional, and spiritual. I grew up Catholic and always had a strong connection and relationship with God. My parents also exposed us to medical intuitives, mediums, and therapists, and we were always open to alternative methods. So after the accident I saw two types of doctors—MDs, but also DOs, who took a more holistic approach. One of these healers was an energy healer I mentioned earlier named Jon Sweeney. Rev. Jon Sweeney is an ordained interfaith minister who specializes in a ministry of healing using bioenergetic therapies. For almost twenty years he has worked as a healing partner with people from around the world. His unique method of healing incorporates his Cherokee ancestors' understanding of natural balance within the universe and their relationship with their Creator. He has helped me heal faster from surgeries, flus, emotional blocks, or whatever else I might be suffering from. His work has made a huge difference in my recovery time, both physically and emotionally. He always says, "Whatever the healing time the doctor has given you, I will cut it in half." It is the truth. I really wouldn't have gotten to the other side of this without his help.

Another wonderful, powerful healer I saw before and after the accident is Julie Walker, an intuitive healer who serves as a medical intuitive from her home base of Wilmette, Illinois. Over the years she has worked with people from all over the globe in the healing arts. For almost a decade she lived in Swaziland and South Africa with her family while she worked with traditional healers from various regions. While in Swaziland, she explored and developed models of evolution related to healing and the sciences based on observations of universal patterns of change.

About five months after the accident, my mom and I thought it would be a good idea for me to schedule a session with Julie. I had a lot of questions, and I knew Julie could give me answers as well as other information I needed to aid in my recovery. Because I wasn't able to drive yet, nor did I want to, my mom dropped me off at Julie's house and promised she would wait outside for me (I was still not really over my separation anxiety).

One of the first things Julie told me was that my adrenal glands were suffering because of the trauma to my body, and that was why my legs were swelling all the time. She gave me a supplement to take that would help them heal. We started talking a little bit about the accident and I told her about my senior thesis. Since I was supposed to graduate about seven months after the accident, my therapists, doctors, and parents thought it would be a good idea for me to finish my classes through independent study with the help of a tutor. This would help me feel more independent and like myself again.

When I first started, it was an extremely slow process. I wasn't able to read much, couldn't fully concentrate or comprehend the material, and suffered horrible headaches. I got extremely frustrated that I couldn't focus. But as time went on, things got a little easier. With the help of my family, friends, and a tutor, I was able to slowly make it through the work. In discussing my thesis, I told Julie that I'd decided to write about the accident—not the details of it, which were concrete and things that everyone knew—but about what happened between the time the accident occurred and when my parents got to the hospital, a period of approximately ten hours.

The one thing that I was still really struggling with was why David had to die. He was younger than I was. "It is just so unfair that someone so young had to lose their life. He didn't even get to experience everything he was supposed to while he was here on earth," I told Julie.

Staring straight into my heart with those piercing blue eyes, she told me, in her sweet, calming Julie Walker voice, "Even though David is not physically here in this realm, he will still be able to do all that he was supposed to do on this earth, just on a different plane. He will always be there if you need guidance or anything from him."

Those words had such a huge impact on my life. I was instantly relieved and felt so much warmth deep inside me. I might not be able to see David, but I could still talk to him and he would still be able to guide me in the ways he was supposed to.

I was very energized by this and had a million new ideas for my senior thesis. I was pumped to go home and write. What shocked me was that, once I sat down to do so, all of it poured out of me in about fifteen minutes. It spilled forth with such ease that I never really had to stop and think. I just put pen to paper and it was almost like my hands were writing by themselves. After a couple of revisions and some corrections for grammar and punctuation, this is what I came up with:

Ten Hours

It was Tuesday morning (October 23rd) around 3:00 a.m. We were driving through Utah near a town called Fillmore. Tony was driving, Jack was in the front seat sleeping, Steve and I were sleeping in the backseat, and David was snoozing behind us in the way back of an SUV. Tony had set the car on cruise control at 90 mph, but then he nodded off. When he woke up and realized what was happening, he reacted so quickly that he overcorrected by turning the wheel too much. The SUV's momentum caused it to flip and roll seven times. At some point while the car was rolling, David and I were ejected through the sunroof and I ended up about fifty feet away from the car. Steve, who was shaken up but conscious, got out, ran to the exit ramp, crossed the highway, and called the police for help from a pay phone. He then returned to the car, pulled Tony and Jack out, and laid them on the ground.

The town we were near was so small it had only one police officer, and the person who answered Steve's call had to contact him at his home. He then had to call the highway patrol and since Steve wasn't familiar with the area, it took the officers an hour to find us. Then the highway patrol had to contact the emergency ambulance unit to come get us. We were all lying there for at least an hour, possibly longer.

We were all taken to a very small regional hospital in Fillmore where our injuries could be assessed. The doctors determined that David's and my injuries were too severe for them to handle and we needed to be transferred to another hospi-

tal 105 miles away in Provo, Utah. David
was airlifted out first. I went next, and
Jack followed by ambulance to Utah Valley
Regional Medical Center. During all this
time I was unconscious except for probably
ten seconds when I came to long enough
to whisper my dad's cell phone number to
a nurse.

So ... what could have happened during the ten hours before I came to?

I gradually opened my eyes and saw a
pitch-black sky sprinkled with a million
stars. I slowly started to sit up but as soon
as I did, I had to lie back down. The stars
were spinning around crazily. I tried again,
and this time I did succeed in sitting up.
This challenge conquered, I had to open
and close my eyes probably a dozen times
before I realized where I was. I was sitting by the side of a road in the middle of
nowhere, and I had no idea how I had gotten there. It was hard to swallow the panic
that rose up inside me until I saw David.
He was sitting up about fifty feet from me
and looking around groggily.

Using all my strength, I walked very
slowly to him, wobbling the whole way.
When I got there, I helped him get to his
feet, although we both probably looked like
we were drunk. Neither of us had a clue

as to what had happened so we decided to walk back to the car and see if everybody else was there. As we got closer, we saw what was left of the SUV. It looked as if a tornado had hit the car, ripped it to pieces, and left it to die. After I picked my jaw up off the ground, I remember hoping that there was no one in that car. We took a step or two closer, and we saw that mercifully there wasn't. David and I kept asking each other, "Where did everybody go?" "Where is everyone?" but neither of us had any answers. I remember thinking that Steve, Tony, and Jack were playing some kind of trick on us. In a second they were all going to pop out from behind something and scare us. I stood a little closer to David, just in case they did.

As soon as we realized we were the only two people on a deserted highway in the middle of Utah at 3 a.m., we decided we'd better get the heck out of there. Somehow David and I knew the perfect place to go. We found a little ice cream shop in Fillmore. When we arrived, the door was open and the lights were on, but nobody was there. We waited and waited for someone to come out from the back room, but nobody came. David and I looked at each other with the same

anticipation and excitement and decided
we would just serve ourselves. We tried
every single flavor of ice cream in that
store. There must have been fifty different
kinds, and we tasted them all. Then we
both made our cones (of course, the big
waffle ones) and enjoyed each and every
lick. As we were putting on our jackets and
getting ready to go back to the car, David
turned to me really quickly and said we had
to go see his family. He couldn't explain
why, but it was something he knew he had
to do. So we headed to Portland, Oregon,
where his mom and stepfather lived.

When we got there, David's mom (who
insisted I call her Amy) had cooked us a
huge meal. It was almost as if she had been
expecting us to stop by. The food was all
spread out like a Thanksgiving meal on a
big long table; there had to be enough to
feed about forty people. She had hamburg-
ers, turkey, chicken, and lots more. What
shocked me was that she had two of my
absolutely favorite things to eat: stuffed
shells with marinara sauce and sweet
potato fries. It was as if she had known me
my whole life.

It was so good to see David's family.
His girlfriend was there too, and she was
so nice and welcoming. I felt as if I had

known these people since I was born. Amy was just like my mom, so warm and caring. She kept making me eat, saying, "Have more! There's more. Here, let me get you some more."

Afterward, Amy let me take a shower in her bathroom and gave me a pretty blue gown to wear. It wasn't the most comfortable thing, however. It didn't close all the way in the back, which made me a little self-conscious. Amy saw my problem and gave me another one to wrap around my back and cover the gap. After David and I both got cleaned up, we all sat around talking by the fire. Suddenly, I got the same urge to see my family that David had had. I just had to go right away. I did my best to convince Amy, but she insisted we stay the night and I finally agreed. The next morning, she gave us each a doggie bag of food, again filled with all my favorites—French toast, hash browns, and lots of orange juice. I had been made so welcome, but I just couldn't wait to get to Glenview, where my family lived.

By the time we got to Illinois, we were both starving! I told David that once we got inside and said hi to everyone, we could sit down and eat. But when I rang the doorbell, there was no answer. I walked

around the house and tried each and every
door. They were all locked. I was a little
confused. All their cars were there, but not
a sign of my family. I couldn't understand
what was going on. My family never did
this. They would always let me know where
they were going to be. Had I forgotten
some trip or mini-vacation? Suddenly I
got an idea. I'd call them on my cell phone!
But when I went to grab it from my back
pocket, it wasn't there. I couldn't find it.
Had I left it behind in Utah?

David and I went to the Starbucks
right down the street. He ordered a latte
and I ordered a coffee, and we ate the delicious doggie bag breakfast that his mom
had made us. After an hour and a half had
passed, we decided to go back to my house
to see if anybody was home yet. It was
weird that none of them were home, but
I didn't panic. I'd just go see Cristina, and
she would be able to tell me where everybody was. I told David that my older sister,
my grandma, and my great-grandma all
lived in Chicago so we could go visit them.

But when we got there, my sister wasn't
home. I had forgotten that it was Wednesday, and she'd be at work. My grandma
must have been at her exercise class or out
with friends because she didn't come to her

door, and my great-grandma was probably
napping because she didn't answer her
doorbell either. I was starting to get really
upset about not being able to see any of my
family, but then David made a suggestion.
We would act as if we were crazy tourists
from Italy and see the sights in Chicago.

We went to Navy Pier, but it was
strangely deserted. The Sears Tower was
so fogged in that we couldn't see anything,
and when we looked at ourselves in the
huge "bean" at Millennium Park, we saw
two people with blurry faces staring back
at us. We ended our day by going to eat
at Spiaggia (the best Italian restaurant
in the city), and then we watched a Bulls
game with courtside seats. Afterward we
went back to my house and still nobody
was home. I started to get really worried
and scared that I couldn't find my family.
Could something have happened to one of
my family members? Was Cristina, Jenna,
or Joe really sick or hurt? David told me it
was going to be okay and that maybe we
just kept missing them. He was so reassur-
ing. He made me feel he would take care of
me and that everything was going to be all
right.

David and I wanted to do one more
thing before we went back to the car. We

both wanted to go to New York and take in a show on Broadway. We went to see *Jersey Boys*. It was my second time seeing the show, but I didn't care; I told David I could see it every night because I thought it was that good.

The coolest thing happened while we were at the show. We must have been the luckiest people in the world because the entire audience was made up of celebrities. It was as if the people in the first ten rows of the Oscars went to see *Jersey Boys* all at once. I was sitting between George Clooney and Meryl Streep. On the other side of Meryl were Brad Pitt, then David, and then Frankie Valli himself. I could barely contain myself, I was so excited. Not only was I seeing a hit show, but on top of that, I was sitting between George Clooney (I always envisioned marrying him) and Meryl Streep (the best actress in Hollywood). To make things even better, at the point in the show when they sing "Who Loves You Pretty Baby," George Clooney turned to me and asked me to dance. I looked at him with complete shock and said "Now? In the middle of the audience? While everybody is watching us?" He gave me a smooth smile and said, "Yes, here … now … you and me." Who was I to argue with George Clooney? I stood up and started dancing with him in the aisle. We danced together for the rest of the show. When the song "Can't Take My Eyes Off You" came on, he sang quietly and slightly off-key in my ear. At the end, he picked me up and gave me a big hug. At that point I felt like I had died and gone to Heaven. I looked over at David, who just smiled back at me with a look that made me feel so comforted. As we were leaving the theater, David suddenly got serious and told me he would always be my guardian angel.

Now it was time for us to go back to the SUV to see if we could find the rest of the group. I was sad to be leaving New York, but I had so many memories to look back on during our entire trip back to Utah. I couldn't stop raving to David about what had just happened. I kept going on and on—I had gotten a kiss from George Clooney, I was the luckiest girl on earth, Frankie Valli still looked great—I don't think I have ever been so giddy before in my life. I was so pumped with energy it was a long time before I noticed that David was not very excited. He was quiet and upset, and I couldn't understand why. I thought he had liked the show; at least, it looked as if he was enjoying it. It was a long flight back to Utah. David was quiet and didn't smile once. I tried everything I could to get him to laugh, but he only forced a half smile.

When we got to where the accident had happened, the car was gone. All that was left was yellow caution tape, broken glass, and a hubcap. I was scared. Caution tape is something you see on episodes of *CSI* or in the news when something really bad happens. But David wasn't scared or even worried. He was very angry. In fact, he was furious. I didn't understand what was going on. Was he mad that Steve, Tony, and Jack had left us behind?

Finally, David took a deep breath and sharply turned away from the accident site. I started to follow him, but he turned back so quickly that I stopped. He put his hands on my shoulders and looked me in the eyes. He didn't say a word, but I knew he had to go alone. I didn't understand. We had been everywhere together. How could he leave me here alone? Here, in the middle of a deserted highway in Utah? Where was he going that I couldn't go with him?

I could tell he was still angry. His jaw was clenched and his breathing was ragged. But now, for some reason, I knew he wasn't angry with me. Then the weirdest thing happened. We were standing face to face when all of a sudden I saw a picture of David at his college graduation float by. The picture looked as if it had been taken by his very proud grandpa who had been sitting in the audience. I looked at David. Had he seen it? He stood there stunned. He had seen it all right. After that a picture of a TV show's rolling credits appeared listing David as "Special Guest Star." Next was a picture of a very nervous-looking David getting married on the beach, with Amy beaming in the background. Then another picture floated up and joined all the others; it was David with a wife and three kids—two girls in pink dresses and a little boy with two holes where his front teeth had been. The slide show continued. Picture after picture showed the big and little moments from David's life. The last one was David—a bald old man with a little gut sitting on his front porch. All around him were all his grandkids. There must have been at least twenty-five.

David and I looked at each other. Neither of us said a word. It was so quiet that I could hear a bird waking up and chirping groggily. All of a sudden David said very loudly, "I can't believe I'd lose all my hair!

I have great hair!" I looked at him blankly and then we both just started laughing uncontrollably. I threw my arms around him and gave him the biggest hug of all time. I closed my eyes and held on to him for dear life. But suddenly, David wasn't in my arms anymore. I opened my eyes and saw my mom and dad walk into my room in the intensive care unit.

7

SPIRITUAL MEDIUM—
JENNIFFER WEIGEL

About a year after I wrote my thesis, I read a book that a friend of my dad's had given him, *I'm Spiritual, Dammit!* by Jenniffer Weigel. It's about Jenniffer's quest to find her own sense of spirituality after her father, Tim Weigel (a longtime Chicago sportscaster), passed away from a brain tumor. She does everything she can to try to have one last conversation with her dad from the "other side." Since I have always believed in spirits, guides, and angels, I was really interested to hear what she had to say about her journey. Maybe it would even help me find some closure about losing David in the accident. I couldn't put Jen's book down; I finished it in about two days, a record for me. She talked about so many things I could relate to—her experiences with mediums, her initial doubts about trying to connect with her father. I was dealing with the same dilemma: wanting to reach out to David but being terrified to do so.

A couple of days after I finished the book, a woman in my dad's office told me she was a friend of Jen's and that Jen was performing her one-woman show inspired by the book. I knew I had to see it. I really wanted to meet her, and there was a good possibility I would be able to do so after the show. My dad, Cristina, my brother, Joe, and I went to the performance. I decided I was just going to approach it with an open mind and see what I could get out of it.

Let me tell you—I sat in the front row completely drawn in for the hour and a half Jen performed! I was so into it; I don't think I took my eyes off her once. It was really fun to see someone who was openly talking about something that is not widely accepted. One line has stuck with me ever since. One of the mediums Jen spoke to, James Van Praagh, told her, in regard to her father, "They're just on a different plane—it's like they're in the next room." This was the same exact thing Julie Walker had told me. When that line came out of Jen's mouth, I knew there was a lot for us to talk about. I had a feeling she was going to be able to help me a great deal.

After the show we waited in the lobby for her to come out. We introduced ourselves and let her know how we had come to learn about her book and her show. My sister and I told her about our background and that we really believed in everything she said. I told her how surprised I was to hear her say the line about friends and family who pass being on a different plane, and I explained that I had heard the same exact thing. I told her about my senior thesis and my ideas about turning it into a one-woman show. We both decided we needed to meet for lunch or coffee—there was so much more for us to share! After we exchanged information, I congratulated her on a great performance and we went on our way.

When I got home that night, I emailed Jen and told her again how much I enjoyed meeting her and that I definitely wanted to take her up on her offer to grab lunch or coffee. To my surprise, she responded right away! We decided on a lunch date and then Jen immediately emailed me back and told me that she had invited Therese Rowley, another medium from her book. I was shocked, and so excited! Therese is a CEO consultant with a PhD in business who can see spirits, read and heal people's energy, and help people understand and release fears constructed during their past lives. Jen talked about her intuitive reading session with Therese in her one-woman show—she sounded like a really cool lady!

Our lunch date rolled around, and of course I was early—I'm always early for everything—but I was *so* excited, I was extra early. I printed out my senior thesis to show them. Jen came before Therese and we started talking and didn't stop. I explained to her exactly what had happened in the accident and how I'd arrived at the decision to use the story in my senior thesis. I told her about all the spiritual and holistic doctors I'd consulted in my life and all the healers I'd worked with over the course of my recovery. We went back and forth, sharing stories and confidences. It felt like we had known each other forever—as if this wasn't the first time we had connected, even though it was.

When Therese got there, Jen encouraged me to tell her the complete story of the accident, so I did. The first thing Therese asked was, "Have you ever contacted David?" as though it was something I might do on an everyday basis. I told her no, and that I was kind of scared to try. So Therese decided it was a fine time—right in the middle of the restaurant—to invite David to lunch with us! At first I was really scared and unsure. I sat there in awe that Therese was so comfortable doing this in the middle of the Salt & Pepper Diner on Lincoln and Sheffield!

She had no trouble "finding" him and began to report her experience of his feelings and what she heard him saying. Therese said that David was very happy that I was finally contacting him—what?! He has been waiting for me to do this? I was a little confused at this point, but I went with it. Therese told me he was jumping up and down and all energetic and smiling. That was David—he was always smiling, always happy. No matter what he was doing he had a smile on his face. When I realized that contacting someone from the other side could be this easy and cool, I really got into it. David basically told me (through Therese) that I had to start writing my one-woman show, or maybe it could be a book or a movie—he wanted it to be huge. Was that just his personality showing through? He'd always liked things "big." Or was he predicting the future? In any case, I knew at that moment that I would start with this book.

He said he wanted this story (his and mine) out there. Therese translated David's words for about fifteen minutes, mentioning many things that I could identify as David's unique communication style or "totally David."

I was relieved to know that David was happy on the other side. When we said good-bye, Therese looked up at me and Jen as if we had had a normal lunch conversation. I felt lighter and more at peace, happy to have had a mini-session with Therese.

Immediately I knew I had to follow up with her and make an appointment. I wanted to hear more from David, and I wanted to talk to her about another family friend who had passed away. As we were walking out of the restaurant, we somehow got on the topic of birthdays. Jen asked me when my birthday was and I told her October 6. She and Therese exchanged a look and they both started laughing. Jen told me that was her birthday as well! Weird. I knew I was connected to her in some way or another. I'd felt it.

8

ANOTHER SESSION WITH
JULIE WALKER

In 2009, about two years after the accident, I scheduled another session with Julie Walker. I always left her house feeling refreshed and abundant, and with a newfound sense of clarity. I wanted to schedule a "check in/up" session with her, something I try to do once or twice a year. It had been a while since I'd seen her and I wasn't yet feeling like myself. I was still living at home and dealing with a little depression. I knew she would be able to give me some insight, something to help pull me up out of my slump. I didn't really have too much I wanted to specifically address with her—a couple of ongoing pains, aches, and physical things, and I wanted to discuss some emotional battles I had been having. But nothing prepared me for what she would say to me ...

I rang the bell and she came to the door with a smile

and a phone in her hand. She gave me a hug and told me to come in and have a seat—she was finishing up a call and she would be with me in a second. As I sat in her living room, I became anxious about what she was going to tell me. She ended her conversation and invited me to come into her office and have a seat. We did our family check-in—she asked about everyone in my family, I asked about everyone in hers—and then she asked me why I had come. I told her about my adrenals and my knee, and explained that I really just wanted to check in.

She took a look and told me my adrenals were still shot from being overworked. She asked me if I was doing anything new. I told her I was still working for my dad. After the accident he had started bringing home little things for me to do from his job at the Chicago Board of Trade. At first he and my mom thought it would be a good idea to give me something to do while sitting in the hospital bed, to bring a little bit of purpose back into my life. Eventually, that turned into me taking the train downtown and going into his office, and eventually morphed into me working for the nonprofit he founded, managing their programs and fundraising. I also explained to Julie that I had started ballroom dancing. I had always been very active before the accident, and dance had been something I loved. *Dancing with the Stars* had just premiered, and a new ballroom studio had opened not far from my house. My parents thought it would be a great way for me to get back into my body and reconnect with who I am. I also told Julie I had been continuing my physical therapy by working out with a trainer.

I sat quietly as she digested everything and then I said, "Oh, did I tell you I'm writing a book?"

She looked at me and said, "Lizzy ... that's it. That's the problem with your adrenals."

I was confused. What did my writing a book have to do with my adrenals?

She explained to me that adrenals help your body regulate things like stress, blood sugar, blood pressure, body temperature, and energy level. Things started to make sense. Ever since the accident I was tired and got stressed more often. I have always had weird blood sugar (I'm hypoglycemic and have to eat every couple of hours to maintain my blood sugar levels) and ever since the accident I had been freezing! She said that my adrenals had been working overtime, replaying the accident to clear the memory from my cells. I didn't know those little glands were so smart and powerful. She explained that since my karma didn't play a role in this accident and any lessons arising from it were not brought into my life from my personal karma, my adrenals were working overtime to clear any cellular memory that I might still have in order for me to completely move on from the event. Smart little things, aren't they?

I asked her about the freezing thing. It was weird— no matter what I did, I could never get warm. I wondered if the fact that I had lived in California for two years could be why I was always cold now in Chicago. In December I had been wearing shorts and a T-shirt on the quad, and now I had to be in long underwear, pants, and multiple layers. She laughed and told me that had nothing to do with it. At this point, I knew I was going to be blown away by whatever she said next. I was excited. Even so, the next words out of her mouth shocked me.

"You died," Julie said.

I looked at her with a blank stare and asked her what she was talking about. I was positive that I was alive and well.

"At the time of the accident, you and David both died and your spirits traveled to Heaven."

I would have loved to see the look on my face at this point. Julie told me that at Heaven's Gate I had felt the most unconditional love and unbelievable sense of warmth, and that those feelings had taken over my body. When I was turned away because it wasn't yet my time, my body went into shock—it needed that warmth and love. She then told me I had been spending the last two years trying to get back to that feeling. Once your body experiences it, it will crave it forever. She explained that since it is obviously not my time to go to Heaven, I need to actively try to keep my body warm. Most people can be warmed with a jacket or a sweatshirt, but it was almost like my body needed to be warmed from the inside out, not the outside in.

Since then I have tried to keep warm, but it is a

struggle. I always need multiple layers, and I always look like an Eskimo, summer and winter. Which you can imagine is no fun, especially if you have ever experienced winters in Chicago!

9

SESSION WITH THERESE

I was so excited about my session with Therese, I actually showed up an hour early! I thought my appointment was at 10 a.m. and it wasn't until 11. Thank goodness for the new Whole Foods that opened up a couple of blocks away. I went there for an hour and walked around and got lost. I couldn't stop wondering what was going to happen. I had no idea what to expect. I knew we were going to talk to David, but I didn't know what else he would have to tell me—that made me a nervous. I was also super excited for Therese to contact our good family friend, Roxy, who passed away in 2003. Roxy had had such a big influence on my life, and I wanted to see how she was doing.

I bought a couple of gluten-free cookbooks and then, before I knew it, it was 10:45, time to head back to Therese's house. My heart was pounding as she led me into her apartment; I was nervous and excited and anxious—so many emotions at once.

She was finishing up a phone call with Jen, but she directed me upstairs and told me to sit on the couch— she would be up soon. I took out my tape recorder, thoughts going a million miles a minute. Soon after, Therese came upstairs carrying a pink rose in a red solo cup. She told me she had never brought flowers up there but for some reason she felt she should. I laughed and told her I do that all the time.

As she sat down and got ready to start the session, she explained what she was going to do. She then said a prayer and asked me to say my full name three times. I couldn't help but laugh a little throughout the session because Jen impersonated Therese during her one-woman show, and she was dead on! After I repeated my full name three times—Elizabeth Rose Antonucci, Elizabeth Rose Antonucci, Elizabeth Rose Antonucci—she paused for a second, gestured to the rose, and laughed, saying, "I guess that is why I brought the rose upstairs today." I laughed too, and at that moment I knew it was going to be a great session.

She started telling me about my past lives, which was really interesting to hear. She kept coming back to my desire to help people, saying I was someone who tried to get people to where they needed to be. I was enthralled by the details she shared, and it helped me better understand some of the relationships in my current lifetime.

After she finished describing my past lives, she asked

me whom I wanted to contact. I started with David. Again, Therese found him with no problem and we had another enthusiastic conversation. Therese said David was wearing a Shakespearean-looking costume and bowing like they did in those times. She said he was talking in rhymes and being very chivalrous. I asked him to tell me more about the one-woman show/book/ movie he wanted me to create.

Well, that was one request he was very willing to fill. He had so many ideas: celebrities who would be in the movie, how many copies we would sell, and the talk shows I would be on. It was exciting to hear all this from him. I then wanted to know if he was okay. How was he feeling, and what was going on with him since the accident? Therese said that he was laughing and told her he was awesome. He was doing theater and having so much fun on the other side! He said that he went on the most fun ride. I asked him what ride this was and he said that when he flew out of the car, it was like a fun roller coaster and it didn't hurt one bit. I was so happy to hear that he hadn't suffered. I then asked him if he'd liked my senior thesis. He said of course he enjoyed it because it was what happened.

David and I finished our conversation and again he told Therese to tell me that he would always be here for me. He said if I ever needed anything at all, to just call on him. If I was sitting down to write and needed inspiration, he said to reach out to him by saying "Lord David" and he would be there for me (that would explain the Shakespearean costume and rose).

After David and I said our good-byes, Therese said a prayer to bless him and let him go back to where he was supposed to be, and she said that the rose was from David to me.

Then she asked me whom I wanted to contact next. I told her about Roxy. She asked me to say my name again three times and then say Roxy's name three times, so I did. I sat back and watched Therese. All of a sudden, this smile grew on her face. She said, "Wow! Roxy is a big energy isn't she?"

I just laughed. "Yes, she always has been, and I am sure she didn't change on the other side!" I told Therese the reason I wanted to contact her was to see if there was anything else she wanted to tell me, and also because I just wanted to check in and say hi. Therese told me that Roxy was on a stage and that on the other side, Roxy was my stage manager. She also told me Roxy was managing David! That blew my mind! Roxy and David knew each other? I couldn't believe it! I now knew for sure that David was going to be okay because he had Roxy right by his side.

Roxy said that I was on the right path, and she was so happy that I was pursuing a career in acting and following my dream because that was the path that would eventually lead me to exactly what I was supposed to do. She said there would be a lot of doors closing over the next couple of months, and that on my way out of auditions I could "mother fu*k the directors," but I shouldn't. I should always keep my head up and be polite because it *would* happen—everything would come together.

Roxy then told me I had to relay a message to my dad. Their birthdays are a month apart and they had always been extremely close friends. She told me I had to tell him to "Get the hell off my stage and let me do my job and get me where I am supposed to go." My dad is very helpful, supportive, and involved in my career and is always trying to be my advocate. So when I told my dad what she said, he laughed so hard he almost cried. He told me that was exactly something that she would say.

As Roxy and I were saying our good-byes and Therese was about to say her prayer, Roxy jumped in and said, "Lizzy, you know how you thought that an angel came in and helped you fly safely out of the car and land on the road? That was me ... I helped you out of the car."

As Therese was saying her prayers and blessing Roxy back to wherever she was supposed to be, I couldn't help but smile. I knew I'd had my seat belt on, but I flew out of the car anyway. Now I know why: Roxy.

10

JAMES VAN PRAAGH

I first learned about James Van Praagh from Jen's book but had been hearing about him for years afterward. He is one of the most celebrated and respected spiritual mediums working today and has helped bring mindful awareness to the subject of communication with the dead. When he came to Chicago, I knew I had to go see him. One of my best friends, Jessica, had lost her father three years earlier and she wanted to go too—it would be her first step in trying to connect and communicate with him. My parents and I, Jessica, and a friend of Jessica's were happy to join in for the ride and see what he had to say. I prayed that she would get a reading. I knew how badly she wanted to connect with her dad and how long it had taken her to get to this space, so going into that night, I really set my intention for her to receive the answers she was looking for.

In a room of about a hundred people, James started the evening by explaining a little bit about his clairvoyance and how he first learned about his gifts. After telling us some stories, he jumped into reading the audience. He began by having us all center ourselves and bring our intention to those we wanted to connect with. I hadn't really gone in wanting to reach out to anyone—I had already connected with David, and I really wanted Jessica to get her reading. So during this time, I prayed to connect with my Nana Nana (my great-grandma) and then said a short little prayer that Jessica receive a reading.

As I was sitting there, the point in my neck where I have a fusion really started to ache. I mentioned it to my mom and we both said at the same time, "Nana Nana" —her neck always used to bother her. I vividly remember her saying that her "old bones needed to be rubbed." I didn't really think much into it. I smiled knowing that she was with us and enjoyed listening to James read the crowd. He told us that whenever he asked a question, he didn't want us to feed him information. If something made sense to us, we were to just say yes or no.

He read about three people in the audience and then he paused and said, "I have someone else coming through. He's a young man, very vibrant, and it has something to do with a car accident … does this make sense to anyone?" My mom, dad, Jessica, and Jessica's friend turned and looked at me. James continued, "Does the number nineteen make sense?" My mom kept hitting my knee. "No," I whispered to her, "the accident was on the twenty-third … this can't be for me."

My mom quickly responded, "Tony and David were both nineteen years old."

I took a deep breath, and just as I exhaled James said, "The car was very mangled and the police had a hard time writing up the report because it was difficult to tell it was a car."

My mom and Jessica both hit me and told me to stand up. As I rose, I said, "Yes." I hadn't expected to get a reading, so I knew something important was coming my way. I wasn't exactly nervous, but my body was shaking anyway.

James asked me my name. He asked me if what he said made sense and rang true for me—I told him it did. He asked, "How long ago was the accident?"

"Almost eight years ago."

"Do the names David and Tony mean anything to you?"

In my head I replied *holy shit,* and into the microphone I said, "Yes."

He continued, "David is here with me. Wow, he's a funny one. He is very happy but he feels Tony's sadness. Are you still in touch with Tony?"

I told him I hadn't talked to Tony for years.

"David would like for you to reach out to him. He knows Tony is hurting and suffering from depression, and he fears he may do something to harm himself. He would really like you to make sure Tony knows he doesn't blame him for what happened. He also wants you to let him know that he is happy and enjoying life on the other side. He is at peace, and his wish is that Tony can be at peace too."

Not knowing how I was going to do what David asked, I assured both David and James that I would pass along the message. Just as James was finishing up, he asked, "Do rainbows mean anything to you?"

I indicated yes and he continued. "David says he sends them for you. It's his way of reminding you he is watching over you and will never forget you."

And with that I sat down. Stunned. But I didn't know how to proceed. How in the hell was I going to contact Tony and tell him what had happened? He would probably think I was crazy, right? Of course. I mean, speaking with mediums is becoming more and more accepted, but it's still not the norm. Also, I was so sad to hear that Tony was still struggling.

I waited a day, letting things settle within me. Once I'd processed and collected my thoughts, I wrote Tony an email.

June 16, 2015—email to Tony

Hi Tony,
I hope this finds you well. I went to see James Van Praagh, spiritual healer and medium, last night and I wanted to share what happened. There were about a hundred people in the audience and maybe five people were singled out who had spirits come to speak to them through James. Since so few people received

messages last night, I felt it was extremely
important to share this with you.

He started by talking about a car accident
and then asked if the names David or Tony
meant anything and something about the
age nineteen. Immediately my heart started
beating faster, as I knew it was meant for me.
David came through to James and had a mes-
sage for you. David told James to ask me to let
you know that he doesn't blame you for what
happened. He said accidents happen and he
hopes that you don't blame yourself. He asked
me to let you know that he loves you and he
wants to help you live your life to the fullest.
James even picked up that my mom was in the
room with me and asked if she had brought
me. I said, actually I brought her. It made me
think of the first time we saw each other post-
accident and my mom told you not to blame
yourself and that David wouldn't want his
death to be in vain. James also mentioned that
David said he knows you are still struggling
with his death and he can feel the pain and
hurt you are going through.

I do not know your beliefs or where you
stand on this, but I feel it is important for me
to pass this information along to you. I think
about you often and am always sending you
love and prayers. I hope you know that I don't
blame you either. There are no hard feelings. I

*have nothing but love for you. Really, the best
way to honor David and what happened is by
living a fulfilling and happy life. I often try to
remind myself of this. Not one day goes by that
I don't think about you, the car accident, and
David. I am reminded of how lucky I am to
be here, and I think that is what drives me to
make the most of every moment.*

*I hope you are happy and doing what you
love! If you have any questions or want to
know more, please feel free to reach out. I am
happy to talk to you about it further.*

*All my love,
Liz*

On July 10, I received a response from Tony. He told
me that he hadn't been too sure how to respond to my
message, but he was going to do his best. He told me
that reading my email brought out a ton of emotions. He
thanked me for sending it to him, and assured me that
David was correct—he still suffers every day, thinking
about what life would be like if that night had never
happened. He thinks about everyone in the car and
wonders how we're doing, but he had been blocked
by fear and hadn't reached out to any of us. He went
on to tell me that he had heard and read everything I
said and he was going to try his best to keep all of it
in mind, even though it was hard for him not to blame
himself since he was the driver. He also mentioned that

he was so grateful that I had reached out to him, as the message from David was definitely something he had needed to hear.

On July 12, 2015— my response to Tony

Hi Tony,

Thank you so much for responding. I have been thinking about you and wondering how you had received my message. It means a lot that you got back to me.

I can't even imagine what you go through on a daily basis. I have been in therapy ever since the accident and it has helped me a lot. Are you talking to anyone? Is there anything I can do to help?

I, too, have run the "what ifs" and "what could have beens," and I think about all the possible scenarios that could have happened that night. It makes me nuts, but I definitely get stuck in that place from time to time. More so starting in the month of September, but I do find myself consumed with them on random days for whatever reason.

I have often wondered why I haven't been in contact with you, Steve, and Jack. I, too, have wanted to get in touch and don't really know why I haven't. I think because it's scary. It's scary to open it all back up again, it's scary to return to that place, and it's sometimes easier to just not go there. I don't necessarily think it's the right choice, but sometimes it's what I choose for the sake of getting through the days. Also, like you, I don't really know what to say. I don't know what I can say, should say, and shouldn't say, etc. It's a vicious cycle.

I would love to change that. At least start to. I would love to stay in touch with you. Chat with you; be there in any way that I can be, questions, thoughts, venting, anything. I know I could use another person who totally understands exactly what happened that night. If it is something you're open to, I would love to chat, email, text, anytime you want.

I am doing well. I have my own theater company in Chicago and we are just about to head into our third full season. It has been a wild ride. A lot of ups and downs but Chicago is a great theater community and thankfully we have been really well received. How are things in your life? What are you up to now? I saw on Facebook you're living in NY. How do you like it? You're originally from the East Coast, right?

Hope you had a wonderful weekend.

xo

I never did get a response back from Tony. But I know that, when he is ready, the conversation will go on. I continue to pray for him each and every day and think of everyone involved in the accident with so much love and light.

As much as I wanted Jessica to get a reading that night, and as disappointed as I was for her, I knew the reason I had to be there was for Tony. If Jessica hadn't gotten us tickets to see him, Tony wouldn't have gotten his message.

11

MADDY: MY ANGEL DOG

As I was going through rehab and my end date was drawing near, I decided I was going to buy myself a "done with rehab" present—I was going to get myself a puppy. I started looking around at different breeders that were registered with the National Kennel Club and, on one website, Riverside Puppies, I found a puppy named Cream Puff. I continued my search, but something kept drawing me back to her. She was a Maltipoo (Maltese and poodle mix) located in St. Louis. I called the breeder, Rebecca, to get more information about Cream Puff and to learn more about their business. I decided there was a reason I kept coming back to this particular puppy and that she was the one for me. I sent in my deposit and decided to rename her Maddy. I waited week by week for Rebecca's updates and pictures. Maddy had

Maddy as a puppy, indoors and out.

April 24, 2008, Rebecca's message: "The puppies are playing longer and sleeping less. They will begin going out on the grass this weekend for Potty Training 101. She loves to tilt her little head for pictures. She is a very sweet puppy."

been born on March 21 and I was going to be able to pick her up on May 26.

As the days went on, I continued rehab and waited patiently for my weekly picture to come from Rebecca, who updated her website and sent out photos after 5 p.m. on Thursdays. Every week, without fail, there were new pictures of my little Maddy waiting in my inbox.

I smiled for the whole day when these pictures came through. Finally, my everyday rehab ended, but I still had to go to outpatient rehab for my neck and arm—I didn't yet have great range of motion. Needless to say, I was still really depressed. I hated depending on others

Rebecca's message, May 1, 2008: "Maddy is doing great and getting very fluffy. They are very playful now."

to drive me places and help me do things. I was so frustrated that I couldn't do anything on my own. I was also still very attached to my mom at this point. Ever since October 23, 2007, I had depended on her to do everything for me—dress me, bathe me, put me to bed, help me go to the bathroom. Even going out with my friends proved to be challenging because I missed my mom. Can you believe that? I was twenty-two and I couldn't be away from her for more than an hour without having separation anxiety!

So these pictures of Maddy gave me something to look forward to, something to put my love and energy into. I am sure my mom was relieved that I had found

Rebecca's message, May 15, 2008: "Maddy was the only puppy that would hold still for pictures today. She is such a sweet little puppy. It rained all day, so they were all full of energy. They are doing very well on the paper training. I am still letting them eat multiple meals a day, because they are not 2 lbs. yet. As soon as they reach that milestone, they will be placed on an eating schedule."

something else to attach myself to besides her. My mom is the most loving, caring, supportive woman there is and she totally understood my anxiety. But at the same time, I am sure she missed her alone time. My dad is equally understanding and as caring and compassionate toward my needs, but I am sure he was relieved to have his wife back.

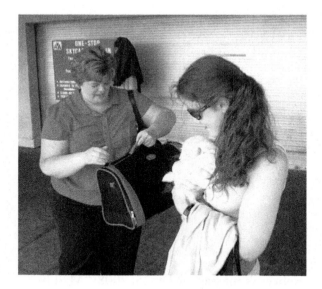

Maddy being dropped off—right out of
the bag.

▲ ▼ ▲

The time had finally come; I was getting Maddy within
a month! Twenty-three days to be exact. I was so excited.
My mom and I had made numerous trips to get Maddy
her things. I was all set ... now I just had to wait! Thank
goodness I had my graduation in between to help make
the time go faster.

The day finally arrived to get Maddy and I woke
up smiling. My dad and I went to O'Hare Airport and
boarded a flight to St. Louis, and I had a smile on my
face the entire time. We landed and I practically ran to

Holding Maddy.

the drop-off section of the airport. I was so excited I could barely contain myself. I could not sit still if my life depended on it. I was pacing back and forth until finally Rebecca's sister arrived. I watched as she got out of the car with a red and black duffel bag and pulled out the cutest, fluffiest, most perfect white puppy.

My dad and I thanked Rebecca's sister for dropping Maddy off and proceeded back through the airport so we could make our flight home. I have never held on to

Getting introduced.

something so tightly in my life! I didn't want anything to happen to her. I knew from the moment I set eyes on her that I loved her more than anything. She was my angel! I couldn't wait to get through the gate so I could sit and play with her while we waited for our flight. Every person we walked by wanted to pet her. People wanted to know what breed she was, and they would just stop and stare because she was so cute! She looked like a stuffed animal.

She was such a great puppy on the flight! She slept under the seat in front of me—it was the only way I could do it, as I couldn't imagine putting a small puppy

Maddy licking my face.

alone in the belly of a plane. She was so quiet the whole time—nobody even knew she was there.

This was the happiest I had been in a long time. I smiled constantly for weeks. Maddy slept in a cage in my room for the first couple of months and then she slept in my bed. I wanted to be with her constantly—I even took her to work with me because I didn't want to leave her at home.

She was a big hit at work—honestly, I expected nothing less. She was truly my angel. She helped me through the times when I was depressed and felt like my life was at a standstill. Because I had something else to devote my love and energy to, I slowly began to come out of my depressive state. Adopting Maddy was

Maddy in the office.

the best thing I could have done for myself. She gave me back my independence. She allowed me to put my love and energy into something besides my family. She started to get me moving again. I took her on walks and to the park, played with her in the backyard—we did everything together. She taught me to smile again. She continues to keep me smiling.

Through all the additional surgeries I had to have post-accident—an operation on my knee to repair my meniscus, a procedure on my shoulder, surgery on my nose to repair my deviated septum—and all the times

Maddy sitting in the car on the way home.

my back went out because of slipped discs, Maddy was right by my side. She loved me and snuggled with me when I felt at my worst. She always came running and brightened my day when I walked in the door. She gave me the strength to go on. Dogs are angels on earth—angels that know how to heal you when you don't know how to heal yourself.

12

GRADUATION

Although I wasn't completely done with classes (I still had to finish two more, which I would be taking online over the summer of 2008), I was able to go out to Los Angeles to walk across the stage and graduate with the rest of my class. I was extremely excited and nervous to go back. The last time I had been to LA was to see the performance of *The Laramie Project*, the show we were researching, rehearsing, and preparing for when the accident happened.

Unfortunately, at that time, I wasn't really present. I was physically at the school, watching the play and talking to my friends, but something wasn't allowing me to be fully grounded and in my body, probably a defense mechanism to prevent too many emotions from coming back. On some level, I think my body and unconscious knew that I wasn't yet ready to process anything. It was still all too real, too raw, and it made me feel too vulnerable. So, naturally, when I went back for graduation I was nervous, excited, sad, and scared to see everyone again. I was hoping that I would be able to fully stay in my body and have fun. I wanted to remember my graduation and celebrate it, instead of having a negative experience.

My mom and I flew out a couple of days beforehand to relax and hang out. We caught up with my old boss, Megan, my friend Jill, with whom I also worked at Mandalay, and my friend Wendy. We relaxed, did some shopping, and caught up with old friends—it was a lot of fun. My dad, sister, cousins, and aunt all flew in later that week. When they arrived we went out for dinner and I showed them around LA.

The morning of my graduation I was really excited but nervous to see everyone—I didn't know how the reunion was going to go. I hadn't seen Jack or Steve since the accident, and I didn't know if I would ever see Tony again—I didn't quite know what to expect. When I got to the school, I went to the gym to line up for the ceremony. Reuniting with everyone, I was actually really happy. To my surprise, I stayed fully grounded the entire time and really enjoyed catching up. I was pretty emotional—seeing Jack was hard for me. Jack had been sleeping in the front passenger seat with his legs on the dashboard in front of him. Both of them were shattered in the accident. I was thrilled to see him out of a wheelchair. His goal was to walk across the stage for graduation and I was very proud of him for doing so.

I took a lot of pictures with my friends, but something was missing. Although I was excited to see everyone, it was odd to just show up for that day. The theater department at Loyola Marymount is small enough that everyone knows everyone and the seniors had all gotten really close. I felt like I had just invited myself somewhere. Even though everyone was really nice and caring and supportive, I couldn't help but feel like I didn't belong, like an outsider.

Anyone who has graduated from college knows that it's supposed to be one of the happiest times of your life, something you will always remember. These friends are supposed to last forever. That wasn't the case for me. I was excited to hit this milestone, but it just didn't feel right. As we sat through the ceremony, I thought about how long and hard I had fought to get to this point. College was never something I loved. I knew I wanted to graduate because if I didn't, I would have regretted it, but I always thought my time would be better served doing something out in the world. At the time, I knew I wanted to be an actor, or involved in the arts or the entertainment field in some other way. I wanted to spend my time helping others; sitting in a classroom was not something I loved to do. During the two hours of the graduation ceremony, I reflected on feeling very happy to be at this point in my life—and feeling even more excited to leave.

Finally, it was time to receive our diplomas. As our row made our way up to the front, I had a huge smile

Dad, me, and Mom at my graduation.

on my face. I couldn't believe I was finally done with college. I made my way onto the stage, saw my family in the crowd, waved, smiled, and walked across. I shook the president's hand and made my way down the other side of the stage. Standing at the bottom of the stairs were professors from the theater department. Immediately I found myself choking up again. I was so happy to see all of them, and they were all very happy to see me. I hugged every one of them and continued walking. I then found my dad, who was taking pictures. I gave him a kiss and made my way back to my seat.

I sat for a couple of minutes and then people started to meander out. It wasn't a formal ceremony; there were people on their phones, talking and getting up and down throughout the whole thing. Eventually I got up and went to go find my family. I found my sister, aunt, cousins, and Megan, who had come to watch me walk. We made our way to the fountain in front of the theater building and the pictures began! We stayed for about forty-five minutes after the ceremony ended before heading back to the hotel to have some lunch.

By the time we got there, everyone was really hungry. I hadn't eaten breakfast that morning because I was running late. We sat outside by the pool and ate. After celebrating with margaritas (which got my mom and me a little tipsy), we decided to take a nap. We were going out to dinner that night with my family, Jill, Megan, and Wendy.

Wendy had done my makeup for some headshots when I first moved out to California, and we have been friends ever since. I of course wanted to see her and have her be part of my celebration, so she came over to our hotel early. She did the makeup for my sisters, my aunts, my mom, and me before we went to dinner. We got dressed, got in a limo, and headed for Dolce, a phenomenal Italian restaurant in downtown LA. We shared many laughs and had a lot of fun—it was a great celebration for such a big event in my life.

The next morning was Mother's Day, so we had brunch at the hotel and celebrated our two mothers: my mom and my aunt. After brunch it was time to pack up and head to the airport. Overall, it was a successful trip.

Me (a little sunburned), Megan, and Jill at dinner in LA.

I stayed in my body the whole time and had a lot of fun celebrating with friends and family, but I was thrilled to be closing this chapter in my life.

13

Not a Victim

In the months after I returned from the hospital, it was important to me that I not be a victim, and I know I couldn't have managed that on my own. My family was the reason I was able to stay so positive and optimistic throughout. I am so lucky to have the best family in the world. Really, thinking back, I don't think I could be any luckier. Of course, I have always loved and been thankful for them, but this type of experience really brings into focus what people mean to you, just how lucky you really are, and who is important to you.

From the moment my family heard about the accident to the moment I came home from the hospital, and even now, they have been so caring and helpful in my recovery. They have been there for me every step of the way. Whether it's days when I need support and understanding, or days when I am able to run and laugh

Jenna, me, and Cristina—Christmas Eve, two months after the accident.

and have fun with my siblings, I really have the best family ever.

They always made me feel normal. They never treated me like a victim or somebody who was different. Even when I was scared to go out in public or nervous about what people would think, they just looked past my neck brace, the sling on my arm, and my cane or walker, and treated me just as normally as ever. (Ha! Yes, family—I know I have never been "normal.")

My family and I and a couple of family friends had been traveling to Mexico for every Christmas vacation for about five or six years. The year of the accident, I didn't know if I was going to be able to go. But my doctors gave me the all-clear to fly again and to be away

Cristina, me, and Jenna on New Year's Eve in Mexico.

from them for a week, and I was so excited. I knew this year I wasn't going to be able to do everything I usually did—parasailing, jet skiing, ziplining—but I was excited just to go on vacation and be away from rehab and doctors for a whole week. They told me I could even take off my hard neck brace and wear a soft one at the pool as long as I wasn't up and walking around.

I had a great time in Mexico and came home rested and ready to jump back into rehab and appointments. The trip was just what the doctor ordered—laughter, good people, and good times!

14

OH, WHAT A NIGHT!

Before the accident, my family and I had made plans to go see *Jersey Boys* the night after Thanksgiving. I had seen the show from the very last row in LA with my summer theater class in 2007. Although we couldn't really see the stage, I fell in love with the show and the music, and I called my mom and told her we had to buy tickets when it came to Chicago. My mom made dinner reservations downtown for the night of the show, and my dad got third row center seats.

Then the accident happened and all plans were called off. I pleaded with my mom and dad not to sell the tickets, to still let me go, to give me this one night out. After days and days of whining (sorry, Mom and Dad), they finally agreed, but they insisted on canceling our dinner reservations beforehand. To put things in perspective, at this point I had only been out of the hospital for three weeks. I couldn't have a conversation for more than three minutes without getting exhausted, I didn't do well in big crowds, I was easily overwhelmed, I couldn't really walk without someone holding on to me, and if I didn't absolutely have to, there was no way I was getting into a car. Yet with all of these obstacles in front of me, I was still determined to go. I knew it was going to be a big weekend, it being Thanksgiving and with family around. On top of that Megan was coming from LA to stay with us and see the show. I knew I would be tired and I was going to need as much rest as I could get.

I had rehab the day before Thanksgiving and it wore me out. But I came home and slept, excited about my big weekend ahead. Thanksgiving morning, I showered, washed my hair, and, except for the occasional walk, napped for most of the day. Megan's plane was delayed (not surprising in winter in Chicago), but when she finally got in we sat in the TV room and caught up. She brought me a bunch of cards from different people around the office and we were able to sit and talk for about thirty minutes before I needed to go lie down again—thank goodness my sister Jenna was home from college and could help entertain.

After we relaxed for about an hour, dinner was served. I walked to the dining room table with Cristina and my mom made me a plate, a small one—I still didn't have much of an appetite. Very happy to be with my family and to see Megan again, I was able to sit at the table for about forty-five minutes: a huge accomplishment for me. Then I walked around the kitchen a time or two with Megan and my dad before lying down again. People came in and out of my room, and we talked, watched TV, and relaxed for the rest of the night. I went to bed very excited, but exhausted.

I woke up Friday morning and lay in bed, waiting for my mom or dad to come get me. Megan and Jenna dropped in to tell me they were going downtown for the day to hang out and go shopping. I didn't have therapy because my parents thought it would tire me out, so I pretty much just hung around all day, watching movies and TV with Cristina, trying to save up as much energy as I could for the show. Around 5 p.m., Megan and Jenna came home, and an hour later, we started to get ready. My mom picked out a dress for me to wear and helped me get changed. She did my hair, and I even put on some makeup! I then sat and waited until it was time to leave.

With the help of my mom and dad, I hesitantly got into the big van. I sat between the two of them, holding on for dear life the entire way downtown. We finally made it to the theater, and I couldn't wait to get out of that vehicle. There were people on all sides of me as we walked into the theater—they said they were running blockade. Everyone was staring and I could hear whispers, people asking what had happened and if I was okay. We finally got to our seats, a task that took about ten times longer than it normally would have. It was about fifteen minutes before the show—I was so excited I could barely contain myself.

I was hooked from the very first note. The cast that night was Jerrod Spector as Frankie Valli, Michael Ingersoll as Nick Massi, Jeremy Kushnier as Tommy Devito, and Drew Gehling as Bob Gaudio. All four main characters and the rest of the cast held my undivided attention for the entire two and a half hours. At intermission my mom and dad told me it was the first time they had seen me smile since the accident. It was true—it was the first time I was truly happy.

At that point I needed to stand up for a couple of minutes to stretch my legs and my back; it was hard for me to sit in the same position for too long. Since we were in the third row, we decided making our way out of the theater and into the lobby would be too taxing, so we walked to the stage and back instead. It was a short distance, but a long trek for me. By the time I returned to my seat, the second act was about to begin. I watched it with just as much excitement as the first—without a doubt, it was my favorite show ever.

Because this was during the holiday season and Broadway was still on strike, they had a mini live auction afterward with the cast collecting money in the lobby. I smiled at Jeremy Kushnier and told him how much I loved the show while dropping money into the hat he was holding.

During the whole ride home, I was wired, even though my body was exhausted. I was so proud of myself to have made it through the performance in spite of all the obstacles. At the end of the night I thanked my mom and dad profusely for letting me go and told them the show had motivated me to work as hard as I could to finish rehab and get back on stage.

That night it became very clear to me that the stage and the entertainment field were what I wanted to pursue. I ended up sleeping the entire next two days and didn't get out of bed unless I absolutely had to. I had exerted so much energy I was exhausted ... but it was all worth it!

Months later I decided to email the actor who played Nick Massi, Michael Ingersoll. He was my favorite; he delivered one-liners throughout that were really funny. I told him how much I enjoyed the show and how much it had inspired me. As an actor, I know how great it feels when people tell you they admire your performance, and I thought Michael would want to know as well. It was because of his show that I worked so hard to get back to work as an actor. I didn't expect an email in return; I simply wanted to give him a little recognition. So I was completely surprised when I received an email back saying that he remembered seeing me in the audience that night and he would love to meet me.

July 3, 2008

Hi Michael,
My name is Elizabeth and I just wanted to write you and tell you what a huge fan I am of the show. I especially loved your character—I think you did a fantastic job! I recently graduated from Loyola Marymount University in

California with a 4.0 and a degree in Theater.
The fall semester of my senior year I was
cast in the play The Laramie Project. *Soon*
after, we all traveled to Laramie, Wyoming,
to research the town and the events that hap-
pened. Five of us had to take a separate car
because we had to be back earlier than the rest
of the group to work on another play, Rocky
Horror Picture Show. *So the five of us left*
on Monday night to ensure that we would be
back in California by Tuesday evening. Early
Tuesday morning on October 23rd around 3
a.m. we were driving through Utah near a
town called Fillmore. The driver of our car fell
asleep at the wheel while going 90 mph. When
he realized what had happened he tried to
correct the car and ended up over-correcting,
causing the car to flip over and roll seven
times. I was ejected through the sunroof and
suffered a concussion, brain injuries, a torn hip
muscle, a severely sprained ankle, and a broken
neck, a broken arm, and a broken shoulder
blade. One of the boys in the car didn't make it,
another shattered both his legs and knees, and
the driver and another boy in the car walked
away with just bumps and bruises.

I was in the intensive care unit for two
weeks and hospitalized the following two
weeks as well. Afterward, I was in a hospital
bed in my house in Glenview (about 20

minutes north of Chicago) for months. Before the accident my family had made plans to go see Jersey Boys *the day after Thanksgiving. I was determined that I was going to go to the show. Now, mind you, I couldn't have a conversation with anybody for more than three minutes without getting so tired that I would need to take a nap. I was never awake for more than 45 minutes at a time. I couldn't walk without someone holding on to me. I couldn't get dressed; I had been wearing robes because they were the easiest things to change. I couldn't sit in the same position for more than ten minutes without getting up and having to walk around. I was easily overwhelmed by large groups of people and lots of noise. And, most of all, I wasn't ready to get into a car, and obviously I would have to ride in one to get to Chicago. With all that said, I was still determined to go to the show. My parents kept saying, "We'll see how you feel," and "We'll figure it out when the time comes," but to me, the time was here—I had been waiting months for this day to arrive.*

To make a long story short, I showered, put on a dress (with the help of my mom and sister), my mom put a little makeup on me, and I got in the car to head down to the city. I was freaking out the entire way, but I knew it was worth it because I was GOING TO SEE

JERSEY BOYS. *I got there and we were sitting in the third row and I could not believe it, I was so excited—my big, gray neck brace and all. I couldn't wait for the show to start. I just want to say thank you for putting on such a great performance and making my first outing such an inspiring one.*

As a theater major, performing and being on stage is what I want to do with my life—after the accident, I had many doubts that I would ever be able to do it again. But after seeing your show, I was determined to work my butt off in physical therapy (which I am still in) to make myself able to do what I love. And I am so happy to say I am now rehearsing a show at Oakton Community College in Des Plaines, IL, and I am ready to start my path in theater.

Again, I just want to thank you and tell you what a wonderful job you did. I could have just sent a short email but I really wanted you to know what that performance meant to me.

I wish you and the rest of the cast the best run in Chicago.
Elizabeth

p.s. I have attached a picture of my sister and me as we were getting ready to leave for Jersey Boys.

Jenna and me before going to
Jersey Boys.

On August 1, 2008 I received this email back from
Michael:

Elizabeth,
I am so sorry for this terribly belated response
to your lovely letter and remarkable story. I've
recently had a family emergency so I must be
brief here, but I'll have more time shortly. I'm
so honored that you made it to Jersey Boys
during such a difficult time, especially when
you had to face a significant fear to do so. And

I am so proud that you're rehearsing (and may have opened) your first show since the accident. Funny, I absolutely remember seeing you in the audience, all these months later, because I remember thinking, "Who drug that poor girl to the theatre tonight?!" If you'd like, I want to invite you downtown for lunch, or perhaps a cocktail. It would be my pleasure to be a resource for you should you decide to think about acting professionally. And, I'm pretty sure that I could get you backstage to watch the show and see it from our perspective. No pressure, just wanted to offer.

Cheers. You're an amazing lady. Please forgive my tardiness.
Michael

Michael and I were never able to connect and make the backstage show work. But the fact that he took the time out of his crazy schedule to respond to my letter meant the world to me. Seeing *Jersey Boys* solidified my desire to get back on stage. It lit a fire in me and reignited my love of theater. Leading up to seeing the show I lay in the hospital bed, wondering if I'd ever make it back on stage again, wondering if it would ever be possible for me. Could I memorize again? After seeing the show, I still didn't have answers to those questions, but I knew the only option for me was to try. I knew in my bones that theater was what I wanted to do. It was what I had always planned on doing and I wasn't going to let this bump in the road stop me from doing it. I worked my butt off in therapy to be able to get back on stage. I read as much as I could to strengthen my brain and memory skills. I knew it would be hard work, but I knew in the end it would be worth it.

15

I have always loved my birthday. I was born October 6, 1985, the last birthday of the year in my family, so when the day finally rolls around, I love all the attention, presents, and parties. But the year after the accident, I noticed a change. The accident happened shortly after I turned twenty-two; when my twenty-third birthday arrived, I felt different. To me, it didn't really feel like my birthday, just another day. My family and I planned a big party for the weekend following the actual date, at a restaurant in the city, and all my friends and family came out to celebrate—we called it "a celebration of life." And that is what it was. We celebrated life and, that night, I solidified my desire and determination to be the best version of myself I could be—to help others with my story and to really start healing all of me, not just the parts of me that were wounded in the accident.

With friends at my twenty-third birthday celebration.

My birthday party: Corey and me.

PART TWO

Lessons Learned

It has taken me a long time to be able to process why God chose me to go through this adventure. I have come to an answer that I truly believe deep down in my core: I am supposed to help others. I am supposed to help them cope, to not play the victim and to believe in themselves. My purpose in this life is to support people through rough times, whatever those might be. Although there are many different ways in which I can lend a hand—through my writing, my work on stage, and conversation—I know that my stories can help people get to where they need to be. It took me many tears, long conversations with

God, therapy sessions, and bouts with depression to figure this out, but with the help of family, friends, and a few other special people, I have finally come to terms with it.

Thoughts on Beauty

For beautiful eyes, look for the good in others; for beautiful lips, speak only words of kindness; and for poise, walk with the knowledge that you are never alone.
—Audrey Hepburn

16

The Struggle to See Beauty in Myself

I often say that I don't have regrets. There is nothing in my life that I would change or do over because, at one point or another, whatever I was doing, I really wanted to do. But if given the chance, I *would* go back and give my younger self some information and advice so I could make better decisions.

For example, I would have been more honest with my parents from time to time. I would have tried to include them more in things I was grappling with, rather than trying to figure out everything on my own. Body image, beauty, self-love, and acceptance were definitely things I struggled with. The deeper I looked, and the more time I spent exploring these issues, both in therapy and on my own, the more I realized that my view of beauty was a culmination of pressures from society and my family, something that I know is true for most women.

Delving into the good and the bad, and seeing how these traits shaped me, took a ton of work. The messages coming from both places were subtle and unspoken but very powerful. Seeing images of thin girls in beautiful clothes on the covers of magazines or on TV with extremely handsome men by their sides translated for me as *this is who I have to be and what I have to look like.* In my mind, skinny girls were happy, lovable, and rewarded.

Trying to decode how my family system affected me was a little more difficult. I see a lot of myself in both of my parents. When my mom and I are out together it is guaranteed that at least once someone will say something along the lines of "Wow, you guys must be twins," "You must be sisters," "There is no denying you are related," or "You are your mom's mini-me." And while there are many things I am so glad my parents have passed on to me and instilled in me (their integrity, loyalty, dedication, passions, generosity, and selflessness, to name just a few), as an adult I now realize and see the glitch in what I was thinking.

I really don't remember a time when my mom wasn't on a diet, and in my pure love and adoration for her, and my desire to emulate everything she did, I soon found that her obsession with "eating healthy" became distorted for me. It took a lot of time for me to find out where this was rooted in myself, and to uncover where my vulnerability to diets and ideas about beauty came from.

Because of what was going on in the world around

me, I learned very early on (probably at age three or four) that food and weight were the "in-road" to be seen as beautiful, lovable, stable, in control, and happy. And who doesn't want to be all of those things? Our kitchen and refrigerator only contained healthy and organic foods, and we could almost never find "sugar cereal" or pop in the house. While now I can appreciate my mom wanting us to eat the best foods all the time, when I was six I hated it. What kid wants to have the healthy version of a fruit roll-up or the organic version of Frosted Flakes? I watched how my mom ate, what she ate, and when she ate. By seeing whatever new diet she was trying, my little brain decided that I needed to diet too. "My mom is so pretty, beautiful, and perfect, if I want to be like her, I have to diet too." Rational or not, I can hear my young self saying these words in my head and feeling them in my heart.

Oftentimes we take on the best and worst parts of our parents. While there is so much about my mom and dad that I admire, I want to evolve beyond my early ideas about dieting and negative self-talk. As an adult, I can now see that when my parents called dieting "healthy eating" or when my mom criticized parts of her body, I internalized it, seeing myself as not thin enough, beautiful enough, or good enough. This formed my inner map very early on. In my mind, to be thin and beautiful meant that I was lovable and wouldn't end up alone. So somewhere deep down I made an unspoken vow to myself to be just that—thin and beautiful—so I could be loved. I would be pretty and good so I could meet a man, get married, and be successful. That was the thread in my psyche that shaped my life, the one that would negatively impact me for fourteen years. And I am so happy that at the age of thirty I was finally able to wake up and break this pattern, to see clearly how I perceived things through my child's eyes and heart. I realized I had to bring this into consciousness and heal what needed to be healed so I wouldn't pass it on to the daughter I may have one day.

I am inviting women and girls who read this book to know that while this is my story, it is also a collective story. In reality, very little has changed in society and I hope that in sharing and speaking about this, we can begin to bring about change. We need to take the power away from these subtle, unspoken thoughts that we continue to put out into the world and instead start to realize how powerful we really are and how much we have to offer.

I remember the day as if it was yesterday. It was my freshman year in high school and I was in gym class. I had become friends with a beautiful girl named Kate. She was about five-feet-ten and blonde and had zero body fat, and all the boys loved her. I was five-feet-seven, had red hair, and had what I considered a normal body type until I saw how many tall, beautiful girls there were in high school. They all seemed to be thinner than me.

Kate and I were talking about what we were going

to eat for lunch and she said she was most likely going to have pizza and Bosco sticks: delicious, massive breadsticks with melted cheese inside. That meal sounded absolutely amazing, but then I caught myself before I got too excited: *There's no way I can eat that—it's so fattening!* Aloud, I said, "Wow, you are so lucky you can eat like that and still look the way you do."

"Oh, it's not luck, it's pretty simple, actually. I can eat anything I want as long as I take one of these little pills before I do."

If the scene were in a movie, this part would happen in slow motion. She opened her gym locker, pulled out her backpack and unzipped it, and pulled out a blue bottle with white writing on it. "My mom bought them for me. They aren't bad for you and aren't dangerous. I just take one before I eat any meal and it blocks the fat. Plus, it keeps me from eating too much because I'm not as hungry ... here, take some." She poured about fifteen in my hand and told me to let her know how I liked them.

I didn't really think too much about it. I mean, her mom had given her the pills—they couldn't be dangerous. No one's mom would give their daughter anything harmful. So I put them in my backpack and ... that was the beginning of a really long struggle for me.

I don't remember thinking before high school that I was fat or needed to lose weight, but after Kate handed me the pills I thought how much better, skinnier, and prettier I could look. I thought about the boys noticing me like they noticed Kate. I went home and looked through magazines, getting excited about how much better I was going to look with these "magic pills." I wanted to look like all the models in the magazines. I knew most of the images were airbrushed, but I didn't know to what extent, and at the age of fourteen, going to a school where I thought everyone was prettier than I was, I was determined to become as "beautiful" as they were.

When I took the first pill, I was equally scared and excited. I woke up that morning, showered, and got dressed just like on any other day. I brushed my teeth, did my hair, and got all my homework and stuff together for school. Then I swallowed the pill in my bedroom before I went downstairs. I ate my breakfast just like any other morning. I felt great. About thirty minutes later I felt a rush of energy. I was livelier than ever before, and it lasted into early afternoon. Kate had told me to take a pill before each meal, so before lunch, I snuck into the bathroom across from the cafeteria and popped another one. I wasn't really that hungry, but I ate some of the food my mom had packed for me and went on with my day. I experienced another huge rush of energy—I felt like I could take on the world. It was a little secret I was carrying around with me and nobody knew. I wasn't really that hungry when it came time for dinner, so I popped another pill and only ate until I was full. I only finished about half my meal, but it wasn't a big deal. My mom and dad were never ones to make us eat if we weren't hungry.

It continued like this for the next week. When I was

on the last day of the pills Kate had given me, I asked her where to get them and if I could have some more. She told me she would bring me a bottle. I was so excited. I went home after my "five-day trial" and weighed myself. I knew I had more energy and had been eating way less than I normally did. To my surprise, I had lost two pounds: two pounds in one week without eating any diet foods or doing any extra workouts! I was thrilled—and I was hooked. And I didn't know how dangerous those things were for me and how detrimental they would prove to be for the next fourteen years of my life.

Eventually people started to notice my weight loss and my changed eating patterns. The attention was invigorating and only made me want to continue on that path. But then my parents' questions and concerns started. What brought about this change? Was I sick? Was something wrong? I had to make sure I hid the evidence well. I would stash the bottle of pills in my drawers or take them out of the bottle and put them in a plastic bag so the container couldn't be found. When people started noticing I was eating less, I had to switch tactics: I ate more frequently to make up for it. If I had five or six little meals a day, they couldn't really say that I wasn't eating. I was. I was just eating less, more often. I was still getting the same results.

Then I started experiencing another side effect: I was shaky all the time. I didn't really understand what was happening. I didn't know if it was normal, but I did know that in a weird way I was happy to feel the pills working. My heart would race, I would feel anxious, and

I would start shaking. And as horrible as it felt, I was excited because I could see and *feel* the results happening. Each week I would lose another one to two pounds.

I thought this was normal. I now know how unhealthy it is, but at the time the attention was keeping me going. I know it was negative attention from some people (my parents, siblings, and other family) but for all the negative attention there was as much positive attention from friends at school and from people who hadn't noticed me before. I was getting attention from boys I never thought would look at me, never thought I would have a chance to talk to—I never would have imagined I was in their league. So I kept it up. When I started to feel the effects of the pills wear off, I switched to a different brand. And thus started a vicious cycle. I switched diet pills every couple of months to make sure my body didn't get too used to any one thing.

When my parents found some of the new pills I was taking in my purse, they told me I had to stop and they thought it would be a good idea for me to talk to someone. I started therapy (the same therapist I saw post-accident and continue to see now). Of course, I couldn't tell the therapist what I was really doing—she would tell my parents and they would make me stop. So I kept it my secret. I found new hiding places. I found new ways to avoid my parents before meals. I did a lot more "homework" than I actually had.

Then I hit a new low. One would think it would have scared me straight, but at this point I was so deep into an eating disorder that I couldn't get out of it. I took the diet pills but I didn't eat enough, so eventually I developed a form of anorexia. My body had no more fat to burn because of the small amount of calories I was taking in.

Things came to a head one night after dinner. I went upstairs to finish my homework and suddenly felt extremely nauseous. My bedroom was directly across from the bathroom so I jumped up from my desk and ran across the hall and started throwing up. I don't know what I was throwing up because I barely had any food in my system—it just kept coming out. After about an hour of me throwing up again and again, my mom decided to take me to the hospital. I was shaking, dehydrated, and as pale as a ghost.

Before I left for the hospital (even in the horrible state that I was in), I flushed all the diet pills down the toilet. I said to myself, "I can't do this anymore." I didn't want to ever feel that horrible again. So I flushed the pills, brushed my teeth, changed my clothes, and headed to the hospital with my mom. I remember being terrified the doctors were going to find the pills in my bloodstream or urine or something. They didn't; I was at least safe from that. But I wish they had. I think it would have had a more lasting impact on me.

After that night I vowed that I was done. I was done with pills and I wouldn't take them anymore. That lasted for about a week or two and then I bought another bottle. I never got to the point of throwing up again, but the other side effects were the same.

This went on for years and years. It was the same

cycle. I would binge on diet pills, restrict foods, and get on a scale every day. Then I would throw out all the pills and swear I would never do it again. When I went away to college it was easier because I was out of my parents' house and didn't really have to be that discreet about it anymore. I still hid my pills from my roommates, but all I had to do was put them in a desk drawer or something. People respected privacy for the most part so I didn't really have to worry about being found out.

Instead of putting on the "freshman fifteen," I was determined to lose it. But this was made harder by the fact that eating a healthy and balanced meal wasn't at the forefront of my mind. Instead I turned to whatever was convenient: late-night beers and easy mac. But I wanted to be the most beautiful I could be at that school, so I lost more weight and stayed as "in shape" as possible.

I was in a sorority that I loved and had great friends. My older sister had gone to the same college and I loved all her friends too. I felt like I had it made.

17

My Weight Struggles Continue

Warning: Reflections in this mirror may
be distorted by socially constructed ideas
of beauty.
—Anonymous

After my freshman year I decided not to return to John Carroll University (more on that later), and I wanted to find a school where I could major in theater. So while I was trying to figure out where to go, I attended a community college in my hometown and finished up my general education classes. I was debating between Columbia College in Chicago and Loyola Marymount University in California. My body image and weight struggles continued during this time. I strictly limited the food I allowed myself to eat and countered that with a couple of different diet pills. I took certain ones in the morning, certain ones in the afternoon, and different ones in the evening. I thought that if I used different kinds of pills at different times, they would simultaneously combat more "fat." This continued on and off until the accident in 2007.

But my struggle with food didn't stop with the accident; in fact, I think that's when it really came to the forefront. I was in the hospital for a month and on an IV for a good amount of that time, and I had no appetite, so I lost a ton of weight. My mom weighed me when I got back home and I was something like 100 pounds or less. I am five-feet-seven and had never weighed less than 138—100 pounds was *really* thin. I can still vividly remember that morning. It was right before one of our showers; I can see the scale in her bathroom and that number on the screen. I was shocked, scared, and excited, and my first (sick) thought was, *I don't want to gain any of my weight back.* And thus was my struggle with food reborn.

Post-accident, I faced a major dilemma. I had to take a lot of pain medication—Advil, steroids, antibiotics—all of which required me to eat to coat my stomach. This ended up causing me to fear food. I gained all the weight back and more. I looked swollen. My mom assured me it was from the trauma and all the pills I had to take, but needless to say, I felt gross in my body.

One morning I was sitting in the Walker Brothers Pancake House in Glenview with my dad, brother, and sister. The menu included gluten-free pancakes (I had been diagnosed with celiac disease in 2006, and in 2008 gluten-free options weren't widely available at many restaurants). I was so excited. My sister asked me if I wanted to split an order and I immediately felt panicked. My brain started working overtime to try to come up with a quick answer for why I wasn't going to get them. I spent a good ten minutes studying a menu that I knew like the back of my hand—my family had been going to the Walker Brothers for years every Sunday after church.

I debated back and forth:

Get the pancakes!

No, they are so bad for you, the sugar, the syrup, the carbs. They have no protein and are wasted calories.

My sister even joked that she could see the debate raging in my head. I ended up ordering eggs. I love eggs and have them all the time, but I knew my reason for ordering them was to avoid a food that in my mind would make me fat.

As it turned out, this wouldn't be the first or last time I faced this struggle. Almost every menu I looked at gave me similar anxiety. Going out to dinner with family or friends wasn't fun anymore—I no longer enjoyed getting excited about food and new dishes. It terrified me. I calculated every calorie and made deals with myself before I was allowed to eat something. I told myself, *I can only eat the cookie or the piece of bread if I worked out in the morning.* For most people, food is a fun and enjoyable part of their day: preparing a wonderful meal, enjoying a delicious bite of their favorite treat, tasting the many flavors. But for me, it was torture.

Then, in 2010, I did one of the stupidest things I

could have done. A new fad diet, Ideal Protein, had hit the market and everyone in my town was going nuts over it. Ideal Protein is designed to help you maintain a stable weight after dieting, through lifestyle changes. It emphasizes education, teaching you to eat "smarter." When you begin the program you are assigned a personal weight loss coach who is there to help you through each of the four Ideal Protein phases. In Phases 1 and 2 your coach is there to help you set your goals and support you on the journey. In Phases 3 and 4 the focus shifts to helping you maintain and stabilize your weight loss and lifestyle.

Sounds great, right? That's what I thought too.

In theory, I think it could work for a lot of people, but for someone who had severe body dysmorphia and an eating disorder, it was absolutely not something I should have done.

My mom was going to try it as well, so our plan was to help keep each other accountable and share the foods we needed to buy. We went for our intake and consultation. In order to begin, we needed to fax a complete blood workup to the office so they could check all our levels and see where we were starting.

The first week or so on the plan was a little difficult. I had made such a dramatic shift in the way I was eating that I frequently had headaches, as well as some muscle cramps. I was losing weight, but I wasn't relying on diet pills so I convinced myself it was healthy. It wasn't something I had to do in secret—my family and some friends knew about it. My mom was doing it with me, so what could be bad about it? But even though I wasn't taking loads of diet pills, it was feeding my eating disorder mind-set. Some foods were restricted for Phases 1 and 2 and they became "bad" in my mind.

My mom and I both did great on Phase 1. We lost multiple inches and dropped quite a few pounds. I don't remember my starting weight—I think it was somewhere near 155 pounds or so—but at the end of Phase 1, I was close to 130 pounds and somewhere around 13 percent body fat. The goal weight I set for myself was 125 pounds, much too thin for someone my height.

The problem was that even when I moved to Phase 2 and we were supposed to be adding restricted foods back in, I felt guilty about them and left some of them out. I was less hungry than I had been before starting the diet, and I absolutely loved my new weight. I loved the way I felt about my body, how my clothes fit, and the number on the scale; however, I loved something that was not healthy and not sustainable. On Phase 1 you are eating an approximately 800-calorie diet. Each of the Ideal Protein packaged foods is about 100 calories but consists of at least 20 grams of protein, so I never felt like I was missing out or needing to add in anything. Their foods also taste pretty good and some even satisfied the cravings for sweets that I had.

I got down to about 126 pounds. Everyone noticed and commented—I loved the attention. I had to buy new clothes because none of mine fit anymore. I was down to a size 24 or 25 in jeans, but now I had to deal with my constant worry and my struggle to stay that size. I was monitoring everything I ate more closely than I had prior to the diet. I definitely had, as my therapist, Wini, and I like to refer to it now, Ideal Protein Brain. I couldn't eat without criticizing everything I put into my mouth. Even though I was eating extremely healthy foods, lots of vegetables and proteins, and nothing processed, I still felt guilty about eating. I would just grab a protein drink or a packaged Ideal Protein food in order to avoid having to cook a meal. It was convenient, and I knew I would be able to maintain my weight better if I did so.

I was able to sustain my weight for about three or four months post–Ideal Protein. But then I was back to the same fluctuating numbers on the scale and the same negative thoughts about my body, beating myself up for anything I put into my system. I know this diet works for a lot of people and I am so happy it does, but I am not one of those people. It did more harm than good for me. Because of my history and patterns with eating, my ideas of what it meant to be healthy, skinny, and beautiful were skewed.

About two months after I completed the Ideal Protein diet, I had a photo shoot scheduled for modeling photos. It was a beach shoot with bikinis and sunrise shots. I was thrilled about the timing. I thought I never looked better. But when I look at the photos now, I can't believe I put myself through so much to get to a certain number on a scale.

18

My Struggle with Weight Needs to Stop

In 2013 I was scheduled to have the shoulder surgery I had been putting off since the accident to repair tears in my rotator cuff. Most of the time this surgery is done as an outpatient procedure, but because of my history, my doctor felt more comfortable doing it in the hospital, just in case I needed to be admitted. As it turned out, because of the titanium plate and screws from my fusion, they were unable to give me a nerve block to completely numb out the nerves in my neck and shoulder. I ended up having to spend four days in the hospital post-surgery because they couldn't keep the pain under control.

When I was finally released, I went to my parents' house to recover. They had planned a trip to Europe with another couple so Cristina was going to be taking care of me. I was on multiple pain medications, several different steroids, and anti-nausea pills. All my medications had to be taken with food, and because I had taken them before, post-accident, I knew that the steroids would cause me to gain weight. Out of all the surgeries I had had, this was the absolute worst, and I was in such an incredible amount of pain that I was unable to sleep. It was the ideal combination for a perfect storm.

After about the third week of being in the same position in the same chair, all while taking an enormous number of pills, I needed to get out and take a walk. Cristina and I decided to stroll to the town center less than a mile from my parents' house. The fresh air felt wonderful.

All of a sudden, as we were walking, I lost it—completely just lost it there on the sidewalk. The combination of constant pain, constant pain medication, and lack of sleep caused everything to boil over. I sobbed to Cristina, "I am so tired of not feeling good about myself. I am sick of taking pills every time I want to eat something. I am so tired of judging myself every time I look in the mirror. I cannot stand the constant battle I have with myself when I go to a restaurant and look at a menu. I am tired of hearing that little voice inside my head saying, *Don't eat that, That will make you fat, You can only have that cupcake if you work out today.* I hate that I'm not able to enjoy any of the food I eat because I am calculating every single thing I put into my mouth."

I think Cristina was a little shocked because it all came out so fast. It was like word vomit that just kept pouring out of me. I continued vomiting. "It is so frus-

First day home from the hospital
post–shoulder surgery.

trating to be twenty-eight years old and not be able to
do everything I want to do. I can't run because of my
knees. I can't ride horses because of my neck. I can't
wear heels without throwing out my back."

Cristina just listened, sympathized, and let me get
it all off my chest. She knew that was what I needed. I
had been holding all of these feelings in and that wasn't
healthy. Cristina wasn't surprised by the words I was
saying—I think she was surprised at how much I had
been carrying for so long. She had watched me diet,

pop pills, and kill myself, and I think there was a part of her that was waiting for this breakdown.

Cristina has always been one of the most influential people in my life, someone I look up to and model myself after. I always wanted to be like her, do things the way she does them, and dress like her. Cristina doesn't wear matching socks, so I started to wear mismatched socks. She is the one person I truly allow myself to be completely messy with. Everyone needs one person in their life that they feel 100 percent comfortable being 100 percent of their true self with, someone who has seen them at their absolute worst and absolute best. Cristina is that person for me. She is so caring, kind, and patient. I couldn't have reached this realization if I had been talking to anyone else.

I made the decision then and there that I was going to stop. Stop all diets, all pills, all self-shaming and rebuild my relationship with food and myself. If I ever wanted to be truly happy in my life, this had to be the next step. Who has the right to tell me that a certain number has to show up on the scale? Nobody. Who has the right to tell me how I should look? Nobody. Who has the right to tell me what number should be on the inside of my clothes? Nobody. It is absolutely ridiculous that I have spent the majority of my life, from age fourteen to twenty-eight, trying to be someone who society tells me I should be, starving myself and damaging my insides so I can fit into a certain size.

I had finally woken up, and it was clear to me that it was time to change. So I did.

Thought and intention are the most powerful tools you have at your disposal. I made a pact with myself and promised myself this was it. I threw away every diet pill I owned, I threw away my scale, and for a while, I cut the tags out of my clothes. The first couple of months were extremely difficult, and getting rid of the numbers inside my clothes let me get dressed without them staring back at me.

Every time I thought something negative about myself, I reframed my thinking. I would say, "Cancel, clear" and reword whatever the thought was. If I was thinking, *God, I wish my thighs didn't touch and jiggle when I walk,* I would say, "Cancel, clear," and reframe the thought to *I love how strong my legs are and that even with everything I have been through they continue to support me and give me the strength to be independent.*

Day by day, my struggle got a little easier. Just by making a small change in how I spoke and thought about myself, I started to see a huge difference in the way I felt. And other people noticed. People said I looked happier and that I was glowing. People asked me, "What's different?" "Did you get a haircut?" "What changed?" I couldn't figure it out, but that's when I realized just how powerful the way you feel about yourself is. What you put out into the world really is what you attract. The Law of Attraction can have an incredible impact.

19

Beauty Is More Than a Number on a Scale, Images in a Magazine, and What Society Tells You Is Beautiful

Beauty begins the moment you decide to be yourself.
—Anonymous

Why is it that we let a number rule our lives? Whether it's our age, a number on the scale, or a number or letter on a clothing tag, it's just silly. To let a number control your life in a negative way is like living in a prison, constantly butting up against something *you* really have no control over. Now, I am all for being healthy and having something as a guideline, but when you start to let that number control you, it becomes a slippery slope. After my breakdown to Cristina, I decided

I was going to get rid of scales. For the longest time I had let the number on the scale and the number in my clothes dictate how I felt about myself. When that number went up, I felt like shit. When that number went down, I allowed myself to feel happy and proud. It did horrible things to my self-esteem and confidence, not to mention my relationships with others and myself. I can't imagine I was the most fun person to be around when my thoughts were consumed with dieting and exercise.

When I made the decision to get rid of scales, I slowly changed my perception and my thought process. No longer was I going to let a number tell me how to feel; I was going to let my *body* decide how it was feeling. And you know what? I immediately felt better. I even dropped the unwanted weight I had been carrying around—not a ton, but I felt the difference in my clothes. And that's how I tell where my body is now. Do I feel good in my clothes, or do I not feel good? If I don't, I eat a little healthier, take more walks, and am more conscious about what I'm thinking and what I put in my body. And if I feel good? I do the same.

How do I handle it when I go to doctors' offices? I don't look at the scales and I respectfully ask the nurses not to tell me my weight. Every single one of them is happy to keep the number secret. A lot of them praise me for it, saying just what I believe—that our lives shouldn't be ruled by a number.

So if you are struggling with this, give it a try. Get off the scale and cut the tags out of your clothes. I have everything from a size 2 to XL in my closet. I have pants and dresses that are sizes 2, 4, 6, 8, and 10, and I have shirts that are XS to XL. How can this be? Because all clothes are made differently; sizes vary. It really doesn't matter what the tag says—it's how you feel in them. When you feel happy and confident, you will automatically have a better day. Take the time in the morning to really love getting dressed. Really feel the clothes on your body. Feel how soft that sweater is. Look at yourself in the mirror before you leave, and smile. Let yourself know it's okay to say, "Damn, I look good" before walking out of the house.

20

FINDING THE BEAUTY IN YOURSELF

Once I realized how powerful my thoughts and actions were, I consciously made the decision to use my power every day. I try to start my morning and end my evening by saying something I love about myself. It's a nice way for me to really allow myself to love who I am and who I have become. We are constantly blasted with images of models who are perfectly airbrushed, perfectly toned, have six-packs, zero body fat, no cellulite, big boobs, skinny waists, and thigh gaps ... how on earth are we supposed to be happy with ourselves when we see these images every two minutes? It is so easy to get drawn into this cycle and start feeling bad. Here are a couple of things I try to do:

See the beauty in whatever image I'm looking at, even if that means seeing how beautiful a model's eyes are or liking the way her hair looks.

Give myself a compliment along the same lines.

Remember that these images are professional and almost always Photoshopped.

Take a walk and notice the beauty around me.

Listen to my favorite music, dance around my room, sing out loud, and throw myself a little party.

Find something that I love to do and that makes me happy. For instance, I always feel so much better after getting a manicure. It's a simple pleasure that makes me feel great.

Whenever you start doubting yourself and feel yourself going to a negative place, do that thing that brings you joy. When you get out of your head and away from negative thoughts, they tend to dissipate. I am a huge advocate of therapy as well. It's one thing in my life that really brings me back down to earth. It's a safe place for me to share all my thoughts, feelings, and struggles. It allows me to rationalize what I feel and what I'm thinking. It helps me know that I am a woman and that all my ideas and emotions are valid. It's a place for me to fill myself up with love. It's something I can do for myself, and I don't need permission from another.

So what diet am I on now? Happiness. Happiness

is my diet of choice. When I am happy and love myself, everything else seems to flow in my life. I am more successful at my job, I am more present in my relationships, and I am a better friend and listener. I am more fun to be around. Once I was truly able to find happiness in myself, my body, mind, and spirit, I saw myself for the beautiful woman I am. I have so much love and beauty to give and share, and I wouldn't be able to do that if I hadn't taken the time to really love myself.

Beauty isn't about having a pretty face. It is about having a pretty mind, a pretty heart, but most importantly a pretty soul.
—Anonymous

Thoughts on Finding My Voice

Maybe the journey isn't so much about becoming anything. Maybe it's unbecoming everything that isn't you so you can be who you were meant to be in the first place.
—Anonymous

21

Drama, Drama, Drama

I don't like to think about the drama I used to create for myself in order to gain attention. It scares me, because it's such a gross thing that I used to do. One part of me is very ashamed of it, while my adult self knows that I have learned so much from that time in my life.

I used to lie to make others feel bad for me. I used to lie to get attention. I am embarrassed to admit this, but part of writing a book means putting myself and my whole truth out there, not just the "good parts" of my truth. That goes against the whole idea of this book. So here it goes.

In our world, we constantly give more attention to the bad than the good. We see this in many places: on the news, it's the bad-cop stories, the shootings, the bashing of politicians, and the hate that receive front-page placement. From my earliest memories, the negative things were what garnered all the attention. For me, it started as a prank and a joke, but eventually it got out of control. It went from playing around to becoming a problem and feeding my need for acknowledgement (gross, I know).

My sisters and I were all in a program with my dad called Indian Princess. It was different from Girl Scouts, sports teams, and many other activities because it was specifically intended to be a father-and-daughter organization. The program provided a wealth of things for fathers and daughter to do together, including horseback riding, camping, canoeing, learning about Native American culture, and building fires.

We always made a stop at Walgreens on our way home from our outdoor activities to get crutches, bandages, and braces, and we all walked into the house acting like we were hurt. My mom always knew we were faking and joking (I am sure my dad called ahead and told her), but we thought we were pulling a fast one on her. How horrible is that?

As I got older, my realization that the "negatives" and "hurts" always received more attention grew and so did my curiosity. In middle school it showed up in the way I spread drama. If two friends were breaking up, I would hear each person's side and then talk to the other person and share what I'd been told in confidence. My adult self can't imagine what I was thinking—how could I betray trust like that? But my seventh- and eighth-grade self loved the fact that both people confided in me, and needed and relied on me for information. I felt like I had a purpose. Similarly, if two friends got in a fight over something, I would take both of their sides, thinking I was doing the right thing in being there for both of them. But really I was just immersing myself in the drama—living it with them, sharing in it, being there through fights, tears, and anger. It gave me a purpose when in fact, what I should have done was *stay out of it*. It wasn't my life. I should have been there as a person to lean on, and after listening thrown the information away or locked it someplace where it wouldn't come out of my mouth again. I was so drawn to the drama, gravitating toward the need to feel needed. In high school this manifested in a lot of different ways.

▲　▼　▲

High school. You are thrown into a heightened state where everyone wants to be someone and nobody really knows who they are. If I could go back and tell my high school self everything I know now, my time there would've been so different. My fourteen-year-old self entered the halls of Glenbrook South High School absolutely terrified. Cristina was a junior when I was a freshman; everyone knew and loved her. She was a three-sport athlete and had a ton of friends, and I so badly wanted to be just like her. I wanted to dress like her, act like her, be as cool as her, and be as good an athlete as her. However, I had (and still have) about as much athletic ability and coordination as an infant first learning to walk.

I tried to navigate my way through the halls while being terrified the entire time, just hoping and praying I would bump into my sister or one of her friends. I didn't know how I was going to fit in. Despite trying hard, I was never going to be an athlete. I was in student council in junior high, so I decided to continue with that. I joined a bunch of clubs and auditioned for the school plays. I literally felt like nobody. How was I going to stand out? Now, my adult self would tell my high school self to "Just be true to who you know you are, a kind, loving, compassionate, and caring person who will leave the biggest mark on people."

If only I'd had the foresight to know that. But I guess that is all a part of becoming your true self, right? Learning from your mistakes and becoming a better person. I had a great group of friends, multiple groups of them. I had theater friends, friends from middle school, and friends from childhood. I also had my older sister's friends who I thought were my friends, which probably annoyed her to no end (sorry, Cristina). I felt cooler because I knew juniors who would stop me in the hallway and say hi. But I still struggled to find my place.

I began to notice what types of girls got the most attention at school. It was the skinny "beautiful" girls, the athletes, and the girls who were bubbly and a little ditzy. Since I was already on my way to being a skinny, "beautiful" girl, and there was no way I was going to be an athlete, I decided I would fit myself into the ditzy category. I thought that if I acted less smart than I really was and boys had to teach me different things, they would like me more. I started saying random ditzy comments, or pretending I didn't know certain things would be seen as "cute." I started to flirt with different guys. My ditzy comments were always met with laughter, slight touches on the arm, or hugs about how "cute" that was.

Around this time a TV show called *Newlyweds* premiered. It followed Jessica Simpson and Nick Lachey in their first year of marriage. Part of the show's tactic involved displaying Jessica Simpson's naïve personality and playing into the stereotype of being a "dumb blonde." I immediately latched on to this. If she could find fame, friends, and beauty while acting that way, why couldn't I? I think this was the beginning of my losing my voice. I thought that if I suppressed and hid what I knew was my truth and replaced it with what I thought people wanted to hear or expected from me, I would be a more likable person. My family tried everything to get me to snap out of it. But it was working to my advantage so I kept playing the "Jessica Simpson" role. I imagine it was very hard for my family to be around me. It kept me very small and kept me from discovering who I really was.

22

Losing More Than
My Voice

I was so excited to go to college. Like any eighteen-year-old, I was thrilled to have some independence and to be moving out of my parents' house. I felt on top of the world. I would be attending John Carroll University in Ohio, where my sister was a junior. I had been there a couple of times during high school and had already met a bunch of her friends.

When I started my freshman year, my sister had just left to study abroad in Spain for a semester and all of her friends were looking out for me. Her nickname in high school and college was "Nooch" and therefore I was referred to as "Little Nooch." I decided to pledge Gamma Phi Beta, the same sorority Cristina was in, and early on in the school year their brother fraternity, Kappa Sig, had a date party. I was really excited to be asked to it and even more excited that I was going to be hanging out with my older sister's friends.

I got dressed, and my date came to pick me up at my dorm room. We went to his dorm, had a couple of drinks with some of his friends, and then headed to the party at the bar. After a fun night of drinking and meeting new people, we were going to head to the after party at the Kappa Sig house.

My date and I stopped back at his dorm in between. One thing led to another and we started making out. I was totally okay with that and kind of into it. But then things started to move too quickly for me. I wasn't an experienced girl going into college, and I was a little uncomfortable and tried to slow things down. It worked for a little while—until it didn't. I tried to stop it, but couldn't. It still feels weird to say I was raped because I can't believe that it happened to me. I was scared, I was vulnerable, and I wanted to pretend it never happened.

When he finally got off of me, he handed me a drink and said, "Okay, let's go to the house and meet up with everyone else." I tried to come up with an excuse about not wanting to go, but I couldn't form the words. I don't think I said anything to him. I felt like someone had ripped my voice out of my throat. So I put my clothes back on, wiped the tears from my eyes, and finished my drink, and we walked to the after party. I found one of my sister's friends there and told him what happened. He couldn't believe it.

A few days later we went to the police. Unfortunately, nothing really came of it. The school sent around a letter (sans names) telling students what had happened and to be careful.

I remember sitting in the hallway of my dorm on the phone with Wini, crying. I didn't understand what was going on. I didn't really think I had been raped because I participated in the make-out session to begin with. She assured me that anytime someone says, "No," or, "Stop," and the other person doesn't listen, that's rape. The minute it was not consensual, it was rape.

The rest of the year was kind of a blur for me. Toward the end of the summer, I told my parents I wasn't going back and I wanted to find a place where I could really pursue theater. It wasn't until recently, about twelve years after the fact, that I shared with my parents what actually happened at John Carroll—I was ashamed to tell them. I was scared that it was my fault, that wanting to make out somehow gave him permission to rape me. I was frightened that they would be mad at me for putting myself in that situation.

That experience confirmed for me how unimportant my voice was, how insignificant anything I had to say was. I still can't believe that my date got away with what he did. I can't understand how some of my friends didn't believe what I told them about it. So while my struggle with being heard and speaking my truth really started in high school, I think it was freshman year in college that the feeling of insignificance really set in. The fact that the college and the authorities didn't do anything about what happened made me feel completely worthless. At times it felt as if I was screaming at the top of my lungs and people were just walking past me and laughing.

What infuriates me even more is that this continues to happen every day and nothing is being done to stop it. Every time I hear a story on the news about a rape or an assault on a college campus—or anywhere—my stomach turns, I get nauseous, my throat closes a little bit, and my heart breaks. This is something that needs to be stopped. According to the National Sexual Violence Resource Center, one in five women is raped at some point in her lifetime. On college campuses, that number is the same—one in five women—and that is *not* accounting for all the cases that go unreported. Rape is the most unreported of crimes; 63 percent of all sexual assaults are not reported to the police. How are we still letting this happen? Schools and authorities need to start taking action. A letter circulated to students warning them that something happened on campus isn't enough. Letting these abusers walk free after something like this is just mind-boggling to me and yet it continues to occur. Where are the conversations? Where is the discipline? It breaks my heart that this has happened to so many people.

I know sexual assault and rape are not exclusive to women. I encourage all women and men who have been victims of this horrible act to come forward. Share your voice. Share your story. Collectively, we need to speak up and make a change.

23

THE BAD BOY

After I came home from John Carroll University in 2005, I was in a self-destructive place. I was still trying to heal from the rape, and I'd started dating a guy named Tom. I wish with all my heart I had seen what my mom and dad saw the first time they met him. It would have saved me years of heartache, pain, fights with every member of my family, and trying to reverse everything he told me I was.

My next-door neighbor and I had a bonfire in her backyard one night and our friend Corey came over and brought Tom along. Tom was a very good-looking guy, a couple of years older than I was, and had a "bad boy" aspect to him that I instantly found very attractive. We started talking a lot and went on a couple of dates, and things seemed to be going great.

As time went on, I began to see his true colors, but

I was blinded by them. He was extremely controlling and manipulative, as was his entire family. His parents were divorced. He lived with his mom, her boyfriend, his younger sister, and his younger brother, who was in and out of jail. He started to get very possessive about what I was wearing, and he wanted me to look and act a certain way. His mom and family started taking too much interest in our relationship and tried to interfere with everything we did. It was a very odd family dynamic at their house. I never felt comfortable around his mom's boyfriend. I met his older sister, who seemed to have her own set of problems and was in a very unhealthy relationship.

His dad lived in the city by himself, and at one point was texting me to go to lunch or bowling with him without Tom. I never went, and when this started happening I confided in my parents, who told me not to respond.

Tom never put me first—I was always trying to win his attention. I was competing with his computer, his video games, and a girl who lived across the street that he had a crush on. It was not a healthy relationship to be in. But instead of knowing I deserved better, I did everything I could to be "good" and "win." I baked him cookies and dressed the way he told me to. I lost so much of who I was by staying in a relationship with him. That Jessica Simpson act I mentioned—he loved it. I think it made him feel like a bigger person because he could correct me when I was wrong, or he could laugh at me, and it made him significant and kept me small.

If I was playing the role of the naïve and ditzy girl, he had permission and the ability to be the smart, strong, and superior one.

I met Tom the year I was at the community college, where he was going to school at the time, and when I made the decision to attend college in LA we decided to stay together. My parents were not happy. But like any twenty-year-old, I thought I knew what was best for me, so instead of arguing about it with them I just stopped confiding in them. Whenever I mentioned his name, my parents said, "You are making a big mistake. He is bad news." At one point my dad even forbade me to see him. He told me if he found out I was seeing him when I was home, privileges would be taken away.

Tom used Facebook as a way to control me. He posted pictures of himself with cute girls, or of himself out at parties, because he knew it would make me jealous. If I went out and had a good time and a picture surfaced on Facebook, he accused me of cheating or called me a slut. We would argue, I would cry, and then he would mail me something to make himself the "good guy" again. It was an abusive cycle that I got caught up in every time.

In the summer of 2007, my younger sister, Jenna, was accepted to Tulane University in New Orleans. We all went out there for her orientation, which happened to fall on Father's Day weekend. I had been staying in LA, working and taking summer school classes, so I was excited to go see my family. We had a blast; it was so nice to spend time with them.

During the trip, my dad and I had a heart-to-heart. I was sitting in the hotel lobby on one end of the couch waiting for my family to come down, and my dad came over and sat next to me. He said, "It hurts me so much to see you in this relationship. It breaks my heart every day that you're still dating Tom. To see you dumb yourself down and shrink yourself into someone you aren't tears me up."

I felt so ashamed I couldn't even look at him. I stared down at my hands and said, "Dad, I'm sorry that you feel this way, but I really like him."

My dad is really good at keeping his cool in a conversation, so in a very calm and loving but stern voice he simply said, "I know you really fell for him, but the relationship you are in is not a healthy one. You deserve someone who treats you like a queen, not someone who treats you like a dumb blonde. I want you to think long and hard this next week and really decide what you want. These are important decisions that will lay the groundwork for the rest of your relationships to come."

Still not looking at him, I replied, "Okay, I will."

"Because ultimately, if you decide to still date him, you will be choosing between your family and him. He's making you choose. He's taking you so far away from us. Can't you see that?"

I was not as cool, calm, and collected as my dad, and I got a little defensive. "He has never said that to me, nor would he ever make me choose between my family and him."

"He doesn't have to say anything—his actions speak

louder than words. Just think about it. Take some time. Sit quietly and really ask yourself who you are, who you want to be, and who you want to be with."

I promised I would. He ended the conversation by saying, "Take some time to think about what you're willing to give up for a relationship and where you're willing to compromise. Are you willing to give up your family? Are you willing to give up who you are to make someone else happy? I will support you in any decision you make and will always be here for you, but I really want you to think about this. You may not realize it now, but this decision will be one that will stick with you and influence your future relationships."

And with that, the conversation ended. We hugged. I thanked him and told him that I loved him and that I would think about what he said.

I spent the next couple of weeks back in LA really pondering our conversation and what I wanted. I knew I needed to make a decision for myself before the middle of July. I was going home to Chicago for a couple of weeks after summer school ended and before fall semester began. I knew I would most likely see Tom, so I felt pressure to make my decision soon.

I wrote a list of pros and cons: the things I liked about Tom and the things I didn't. I talked to a couple of friends, my therapist, and myself.

Corey and I had lost touch when Tom and I started dating. Tom didn't want me to be friends with Corey because he was jealous of our friendship, even though Corey had introduced Tom and me. Tom told me Corey had a crush on me and secretly wanted to date me. Some facts: I actually helped set up Corey with his then girlfriend, now wife, whom he had been dating for over five years at the time. So clearly there was absolutely nothing for Tom to worry about. I had known Corey since about fourth grade. He was like a brother to me.

I decided to reconnect with Corey. I nervously found Corey's contact information in my phone and took a deep breath before I pressed the call button.

To my surprise (I hadn't been a very good friend lately), he answered the phone. "Hello …?" he asked in an awkward and curious way.

I was a little hesitant and quiet, but said, "Hey, I know it's been a long time, sorry for the random call … How are you?"

Corey told me he was really enjoying college and being in Virginia, and then directly asked me what I wanted and why I was calling.

"I just got home from New Orleans for Father's Day and Jenna's orientation—she's going to Tulane—and I had this conversation with my dad … I need your advice."

I was expecting him to hang up on me; he had no reason to help me out. I hadn't talked to him in a while, and I had completely disregarded his feelings—I just did what Tom told me to do.

"Clearly, you know how my dad feels about Tom. He hates that I've been dating him for a year and a half, and basically said he knows I'm not the same person I was before dating him—that I've changed, and not for the better. He said I've been neglecting the family and my relationships with others."

"Well, I agree with him. I mean we haven't spoken in a year and a half and we used to be best friends."

I tried to apologize, but really, there wasn't much to say. I felt horrible, and there was nothing I could do about it. I said, "I know, I am so sorry about that. It is totally my fault. I can try to blame some of that on Tom, but that would just be making excuses. It's my fault. I am so deeply sorry."

Corey thanked me for apologizing, and then asked me again why I was calling. I explained to him that I had made a list of pros and cons. I told him I knew I needed to end things with Tom, but I wasn't sure exactly how to do it. "So I need your help," I said. "He is extremely attached to me, and I know he's going through a rough time with his family and at school, so I just need your advice."

Corey stayed quiet for about a minute and then said, "Okay, so just call him. Explain to him that you are done with the relationship. It's too hard to do long distance, you don't feel he treats you right, and you're ready to focus on your career and move on. Call him, be kind, listen to what he has to say, and then call me back."

See why Corey is my best friend? I hadn't talked to him in almost two years and he was still there for me, 100 percent. No questions asked.

Now came the tough part. I had to call Tom.

I was pacing as I dialed his number. Part of me was

hoping he wouldn't pick up the phone, while another part was hoping it would be an easy conversation. I had walked to a point on campus that overlooked the city below and taken a seat on the bench. I think the phone rang once before he picked up. A rush of fear came over me.

"Hey, do you have a second to chat?"

"Yeah, what's up? How was New Orleans?" He sounded like he was in a pretty good mood, and for a minute I thought everything was going to be okay—I could do this. I told him how much I loved New Orleans, how great it was to see my family, and how cool the school was.

He said, "Babe, that's great. I miss you—I can't wait to see you when you come home. Why didn't you send me pictures from your New Orleans trip?"

I took a deep breath and just dove right into it. "Well, that's kind of why I am calling... So ... here's the deal. I'm going to do my best to make sense right now ... I'm not going to be seeing you when I get back to Chicago. I don't think we should see each other anymore. I really need to focus on my career, my life, and myself.

"You know things have been rough for a couple of months now. We've fought a lot, the long distance is just too hard, and I've really hurt a lot of people while we've been dating. I've lost friends, taken steps back in my relationships with my family, and lost a lot of myself. I can't keep this up. I'm not myself anymore, and I really don't like the person I have become. I'm not blaming you for any of this. I just think it's time that we break up."

I heard silence and then a lot of sighs. "Um … okay … why … where is this coming from?"

I stood up and started pacing again. I tried to explain the best I could. "I've been doing a lot of thinking over the past couple of weeks since I got back from New Orleans and I think it's time for me to start thinking about me."

As I was finishing my sentence, he cut me off. "Your dad told you to do this, didn't he? Are you talking to Corey again? I know they told you to do this. They both hate me. I can't believe you're doing this. I just don't know what I'm going to do. I'm not happy right now—you know I'm depressed. You're doing this on purpose."

Then he accused me of cheating on him and asked me if there was someone else. He called me a lot of bad words. Finally I cut him off and just said, "No, Tom, stop. I am not seeing anyone else. Nobody else told me to break up with you. This is my decision. I am sorry you feel that way. I wish you all the best."

Now I could hear him pacing back and forth. He said, "If you wanted what's best for me, you wouldn't break up with me. You know I love you. I love you so much and would do anything for you. We are supposed to be together. You know that. Let me come out to LA and see you, and you'll see that we're supposed to be together."

I told him he wasn't coming here—and that was when he threatened me. "You can't tell me I can't come. Are you not going to open the door if I do?"

I told him to cut it out, that it was over and that

was it. I heard a door open—now it sounded like he was walking outside somewhere. He started breathing heavier and heavier and then told me he was standing on top of something, a cliff maybe, and he was going to jump. His last words to me were, "You'll be sorry … this is your fault."

Then the line went dead. I took a deep breath. My hands were shaking. I tried to tell myself that it wasn't true and it wouldn't happen—he wasn't going to kill himself. All of a sudden, a huge wave of panic and guilt came over me, and I just sat and stared for a couple of minutes. My mind was racing and I couldn't collect my thoughts.

I called Corey back. "Hey … that didn't go so well …"

"Are you okay?" Corey asked.

"I'll be fine. He was really upset and he said I would be sorry and it was my fault. I don't really know what he was talking about. I know he's depressed and not in a good place—his family is crazy right now."

Corey tried to explain to me that Tom had always been overly dramatic and that he was just trying to get me to change my mind. "Whatever happens," he said, "you know it's not your fault. He isn't going to do anything—he just wants to make you feel bad in order to make you take him back. Trust me. I've known him for a long time. This is how he is."

As Corey was saying this, my phone buzzed. It was a text message from Tom's older sister. I read it to Corey. It said, *I can't believe you broke his heart. You know how much he loves you. Do you know he says he's going to kill himself? If he does, it is all your fault. You're such a bitch.* I started to freak out a little bit. "Um, Cor—what do I say to this?"

Corey told me to say nothing, to just ignore her. "It's none of her business anyway. You know his whole family will start contacting you. I'll stay on the phone with you. Let me know what else she says."

Just then another text message came through from Tom's sister: *Heartless bitch.* At that, Corey just started laughing. "Well, she needs to get a life and stay out of yours," he said.

Corey stayed with me for about an hour that night, going back and forth between all the different messages, phone calls, and threats I was receiving from Tom and his family. Eventually I told Corey I was just going to turn my phone off and go to bed. I told him I wasn't going to check my email or Facebook and I would call him in the morning. I thanked him profusely, told him I loved him, and hung up.

I made one more phone call before I went to bed. I called my dad and told him what was going on. I thanked him for talking some sense into me and told him I loved him.

My dad said, "Honey, just know he's going to say a lot of things in the next couple weeks. He'll try anything to get you back. He'll lie. His family will contact you. They'll play into the drama of the situation—they love drama. Know that none of it has any truth to it. Tom will not harm himself. And if he does—which he won't—it is absolutely not your fault. I love you. Turn off your phone and call me in the morning."

My dad was right; the drama continued for about a week. I got messages from his younger sister, his older sister, his mom, his dad, emails, Facebook messages, and voicemails. I went home and avoided him at all costs. He knew I was there, and he drove by my parents' house to try to see me and talk. One time his sister came by the house. My dad had to tell her to leave.

24

Finally Making the Choice to Do Things for Me

Optimist: Someone who figures that taking a step backward after taking a step forward is not a disaster, it's a cha-cha.
—*Robert Brault*

My parents have always said I was the best baby. I never cried; I was happy. I ate, slept, pooped, and giggled. My older sister, on the other hand, was the opposite. She came out colicky. She screamed all the time and didn't really sleep much. So I was born "good." I was born not making waves, a pattern that continued until recently. I am constantly amazed by my sister's ability to always speak her truth—to say how she's feeling when she's feeling it, and to stand in her power. It's the place I strive to get to, and I am finally starting to make some progress.

It wasn't until recently that I really learned how harmful it is to discount yourself. Making decisions based on the wants of others, putting their needs over my own—I didn't realize how disruptive this was to my happiness, my sanity, and myself. Throughout therapy I made connections between the time I was a baby and now. I figured out why I came out a "good" baby and delved into why my subconscious felt like I couldn't make waves or cry when I needed something. It was time to grow my baby up, time to take the necessary steps to bring out my true voice.

So I practiced. Starting with family members and close friends, I really thought about questions and opinions before coming up with answers and decisions. Did I actually want to go to a movie with this person? Did I truly want to eat at this restaurant? Where did I want to go? What did I want to do? Once I felt like I had some solid ground, I started implementing this practice in relationships. *Ugh*—so scary and so hard. Man, I definitely took a couple of steps back. All the questions came flooding in again: What if he doesn't agree with me? What if I'm wrong? What if I made him so mad he left? So I fell back into my "Good Girl" ways and being a pleaser.

25

CHASE

Always speak the truth, even if your
voice shakes.
—*Anonymous*

The year 2013 was going great. I had recently bought a condo in Chicago, I was entering my first full season with my production company, and I had just started dating Chase, whom I had met on Match. com. He was very nice, came from a good family, had a great job—he was perfect. Our first week, we spent six out of the seven days together. It was really fun, new, and exciting. Late nights, lunches during workdays, dinners after work, drinks after my show ... we found time to be together.

My birthday arrived shortly after we started dating, and he took me to dinner and to see *The Book of Mormon*. During dinner we decided we should take a trip. My friends thought I was crazy. They told me it was too soon, that I didn't know enough about him. My thought—why? Who says it's too soon? Who makes up those rules? And why do I have to follow them?

So we went to Florida. We had the best time. We talked, we laughed, he shared things, I shared things—it was great. Shortly after coming home, he invited me to a Notre Dame football game, where I met his entire family and a lot of his extended family as well. We tailgated, ate, drank, and had fun. Of course, I was nervous, but so excited. Things were going great. We loved being together, whether we were going out or staying in.

Shortly after the new year, we planned another trip to Florida. We knew that beginning in February our lives were going to be crazy. I had a new play starting, and he was studying for the second portion of his CFA.

This trip was different. I could feel him getting distant and pulling away. We argued for the first time. There were no late nights that turned into mornings on this trip. He claimed he was just stressed and nervous about the CFA—he had promised himself he wouldn't be in a relationship again when studying for it because the last time had been awful. He and his previous girlfriend ended up hating each other. I questioned him about this, bringing up such points as the fact that I wasn't her, and we were both busy; I had rehearsal five days a week. It felt good to press him: *Authentic Elizabeth: 1, Good Girl: 0.*

He started talking like things were ending. I felt like I was losing him. Little did I know that I had already lost him way before this Florida trip. He had become a little more distant in texts, in conversations, on our date nights, but I continually made excuses for him in my head: he was in the middle of moving, he was starting to study for his CFA, and he was busy at work. I told myself anything to rationalize why he was becoming more distant—instead of actually talking to him.

In Florida, we made a deal that we would play things by ear. If it got too hard for either of us, we would be honest and let the other person know. This was obviously the universe testing me. When we got home, he texted me less and less, didn't call … and what did I do? I fell right back into the same pattern. *Authentic Elizabeth: 1, Good Girl: 1.* I accepted his excuses and even made excuses for him. I told everyone, including myself, "He has friends, family, and work he has to balance. He has to take the little free time he has and split it between others and me. He's studying. He's furthering his career. I should be happy he takes his job so seriously." Blah, blah, blah. *Authentic Elizabeth: 1, Good Girl: 2.*

With every excuse, I was falling further back into the old pattern. Finally we went out again; it had been a week and a half since we had last seen each other. We went to dinner and a movie. I think I knew it was over, but I didn't want to accept it. I sent him text messages every morning—have a great day, good morning—little notes to let him know I was thinking about him. I baked cookies, made him dinner, and did whatever other little things I could think of to help him de-stress.

I know some of this is just inherent to who I am

and my nature—I like doing things for others. I like putting others before myself. I can be selfless, but in this situation, it was harmful for me: I expected (or thought) things would happen in return. After taking a deeper look at what I was doing and what was happening, and after many chats with Wini, I came to realize that there was a part of me that felt, *If I bake him cookies, if I show him I will always be there, if I say how high when he says jump, he will want to be with me.*

It wasn't until a couple of months after we broke up that I realized how hurtful this was and how small it made me. What was tricky was that I didn't realize I was doing anything wrong until I figured out *why* I was doing it. My actions were being driven by what *he* would think of me and how *he* would react—this is what was keeping me stuck in the old pattern. So my *Good Girl* was really driving what I thought was my good nature. *Authentic Elizabeth: 1, Good Girl: 3.*

With each relationship I've been in, this has gotten easier for me. I have been better able to stand up for myself, ask for what I want, and speak to what I need. But it's a constant battle. And just when I think I've won, the universe comes and smacks me in the face, reminding me that I am always a work in progress.

26

My Thirtieth Birthday

I recently turned thirty and the month leading up to my birthday was probably the worst ever. In my family, we have what's called "birthday season"—it starts August 18 with my mom's and goes until October 6 with mine. Between those dates, much of our extended family celebrates their birthdays as well. Growing up, it was the hardest time for me because I always longed for it to be my turn. I just wanted to be the center of attention and to open my presents. As I've grown older, though, I have come to seriously *love* birthday season. It's one of my favorite times of the year. I have learned to truly enjoy celebrating with others and sharing in their day.

But this year was different. I started dating John in the middle of May and things were great. He came to see a play I was in (he made it through my castmates' interrogations), I met a bunch of his friends (I made it through *their* interrogations), and I truly fell hard for him. We spent a lot of time together and just enjoyed each other's company. He was really funny, kind, generous, and caring. He was one of four children as well and had a great relationship with his family, which was important to me since I would do anything for mine.

August rolled around and birthday season was approaching with a lot of family parties, dinners, and events. John and I were planning to see a movie in the park, *The Sandlot*, which was a favorite of both of us. All of his siblings were going to be there and I was super excited to meet them—I had met one of his sisters before at the Blackhawks Stanley Cup parade and rally, but we didn't really have a chance to chat. We were going to have a picnic, and I asked what I could bring. He said his sister had it covered, but I brought s'mores anyway. We had a wonderful time, and his family couldn't have been nicer.

A couple of days later, we went to see a play a friend of mine was directing. I knew that after the play I was going to have to talk to John.

Here's the thing. When we were together, I felt on top of the world. But he wasn't a texter or caller, and when I didn't hear from him for a couple of days, I started to feel really distant and doubtful of our relationship. I haven't always been completely honest about how I've felt, and it's only in the past couple of years that I've really been able to use my voice in relationships. So I was terrified to have this conversation, but I knew I had to—I'd had a lump in my throat for days and had been crying randomly.

After the play, we went to get a bite to eat. I chickened out and didn't bring anything up. But afterward, when we were walking around the neighborhood, I finally said, "Hey, can I talk to you about something?"

Of course he had no problem doing so. I brought up how I was feeling and what was going on for me. He said this wasn't the first time he had heard something like this. We continued talking for close to two hours and I felt great afterward. He was honest about not being a big texter and not feeling the need to check in every day. I was honest about the fact that I *did* need that type of communication in a relationship and reassurance that he cared and was thinking about me. He asked what I needed and I told him; I asked what he needed and he told me.

John said there is always a point in a relationship where it's time to see if the two of you can make your different personalities and emotional needs work together. I agreed, and we decided to stay open and honest with each other and see what happened. We walked back to my car (he had ridden his bike) and he asked me if I wanted to come over for a bit.

On the car ride to his house, my dad called and I filled him in a little bit about the conversation. He said, "Why don't you ask him if he wants to join us at the Bears game for Mom's birthday?" The Bears were playing the Miami Dolphins and we were surprising my mother with tickets. She had grown up in Miami and was a big Dolphins fan. My family had been dying to get to know John, and my younger sister and her husband were going to be in town, so it would be a perfect chance for him to meet everyone.

When I brought up the idea, he said he didn't know. He was up against a deadline at work, but maybe we could all get together after the game for a drink. The next day I felt great. I was so happy to have had our conversation and to have things out in the open. I didn't talk to him on that Monday but actually felt super connected to him.

On Wednesday I went to see a play with a couple of friends while he had his sister's birthday dinner. I got a text from him around 8 p.m. while I was at the show, asking me if he could swing by later. I told him I probably wouldn't be home until about 9:30 or so but he was more than welcome to stop by.

I had a feeling this was the end.

I knew from the moment he walked through the door that he was going to end things. We decided to take a walk around the park by my house and talk. He explained to me that he couldn't give me what I needed emotionally. I kept quiet until he had his chance to explain everything. I then told him I just didn't understand and didn't want it to end. I truly still don't understand the feeling of not needing or wanting to talk every day to the person you are dating. I don't think I will ever understand that. It isn't who I am or how I operate. He said it felt like "small talk" and he doesn't like small talk.

I explained to him that when I send a text asking, "Hey, how are you?" or "Hey, how's your day going?" it isn't small talk. I wouldn't ask if I wasn't truly interested or didn't care—I'm not a fan of small talk either. I ask questions because I want to know, not because I just want to make conversation. So there were a lot of tears on my end, a lot of questions, a lot of sitting in silence because we knew this would probably be the last time we would see each other.

When I was ten or eleven, I was convinced I would be married at twenty-seven and starting a family by thirty. To a ten- or eleven-year-old, twenty-seven and thirty sound very old. So there was a very real part of me that was super disappointed that this was not going to be the case.

The breakup with John really shook me up. I spent a couple of weeks alone, feeling depressed. I couldn't find any motivation to do anything—I didn't want to go to any celebrations, family functions, or events. I didn't want to be with friends. I had been depressed after the accident and I had hoped I would never go through it again.

About a week after my breakup, I went to see Wini and had a major meltdown. I needed that huge release of emotion. It ultimately came out that I felt like a failure in life.

Now, to many who know me, this would sound

ridiculous. I was thirty years old, owned a condo, and had started my own extremely successful theater company. I had just received my real estate license and had a lot of other projects and things that I was working on. To many, this would seem like success. And while I did realize how much I had achieved in my life, I was missing one of the things I desired most—a relationship. I was ready to be married and start a family. Because this was missing, I felt like a failure. I had failed my ten-year-old self, who was convinced I would be married by this point.

Facing the fact that you are not where you thought you would be in life is one of the most difficult things you may ever have to do. It is depressing. It's hard to see and know you want something so badly but don't really have control over it. I knew I wasn't willing to settle for anything less than what I wanted and needed in a relationship, so it was a waiting game that I couldn't speed up.

When I told one of my very good friends, also named Elizabeth, how I felt about where I was in my life, she didn't try to make me feel better or make it okay. She just validated where I was at, and that it is something that is very hard to go through. That was probably one of the best things anyone could have done for me.

My family and friends were incredible during this time. I literally locked myself in my apartment and didn't do anything for about three weeks. I didn't want to talk to anyone, see anyone, or do anything.

Opening night for my company's fall play fell on my actual birthday. I wasn't performing in this play, so my mom, dad, Cristina, and I went to dinner beforehand. I didn't really want to do anything and wasn't feeling like I wanted to *celebrate*. I felt like I had nothing *to* celebrate. Dinner was kind of a blur for me. I was sitting there with my family and they were talking, but I felt super distant. I felt like I didn't belong. I felt like I was hearing them through earmuffs. It came time for dessert and, of course, my mom and dad had told our waitress it was my birthday, so out came a candle. They sang "Happy Birthday" and I made a wish (one that Wini and I had come up with earlier that day) and blew out the candle. No more than three seconds later, I lost it. I was bawling. It was like someone had opened the floodgates. I don't remember much of what was said to me. I felt my mom and dad hugging me, telling me it would be all right, and then my mom said something that would stick with me: "Feel the feelings."

Feel the feelings. Too many times we try to hide how we are actually feeling. We go through our day with armor on, trying to put on an act and a façade so people don't actually see what we're going through. I am most definitely one of those people. I try to always be strong, have a smile on my face, and make it through the day. For the first time in my life, there was absolutely no way I was going to be able to do that. People kept saying things like, "What's going on? Is there something wrong? Is everything all right? You seem different."

I was *feeling the feelings*. I had no energy or strength, nor did I care to put on an act. I was sad. I was sad I wasn't where I wanted to be in life. I was sad that John and I had broken up. Getting out of bed was a struggle. Getting myself up, dressed, and out the door to whatever I had to do that day was a struggle. But the weeks went on and things slowly got easier, thanks to morning walks with my mom, texts with my sisters, hugs from my dad, and thoughts from a few good friends.

About a month after my birthday and almost three months after my breakup with John, I started to feel like myself again. It was easier to go about my day. It was easier to accept where I was in life and to know that things have a way of working themselves out. I knew (although I still doubted) that there was someone out there for me and that I would find him. I learned a lot about what I wanted and needed in a relationship and what I am absolutely not willing to compromise on. For that, I am a stronger person.

27

LEARNING TO SAY NO TO OTHERS AND YES TO MYSELF

I didn't learn how to say no to others and yes to myself until after my breakup with John. I think this goes along with me constantly battling my *Good Girl*.

I have the capacity to do a lot. I know I can take on multiple projects, help people out with things they may need, run errands for them, and lots more. I usually do these things because I love the people I'm doing them for. It seems like what I *should* be doing. But it's a pattern, and I get most confused about it when my family asks me to do things. They are family, for goodness sakes; of course I would do anything they ask or need. And yet, while I think this is true and how it should be with family, there is a fine line for someone who is battling an old pattern.

One morning following my birthday I was on one of my long walks with my mom. (And when I say long, I mean long; the day after my breakup we walked eight miles. I just kept going. I was in too much pain to think or care.) On this morning as we walked I was telling her about a job offer I had gotten to teach improv to little kids. I had started doing that earlier in the year and really enjoyed it. The kids were adorable, my boss was great, and I *loved* what the company stood for. I loved how much confidence the class gave the kids and what a great equalizer it was. But as much as I adored teaching there, and as much as I wanted to help the person who offered me the job, I knew it wasn't the right choice for me.

I debated back and forth with my mom for a bit:

"But Mom, what if she can't find a replacement teacher?

"She's getting married, and I know she'll need the help in a couple months covering those classes.

"Am I not staying true to my word?

"No, I didn't sign a contract saying I'd work for a certain period of time ... but ..."

My mom responded pretty much the same way after every point I made:

"But honey, is it really what you want to do?

"Honey, is it going to make you happy?

"Honey, don't you have other things lined up that are going to feed you more than this will?"

Since I had made an agreement with myself to start making choices for me and not for others, I declined the offer to continue teaching. It was hard. It was difficult to disappoint someone—*but it was better than disappointing myself.* Saying no would allow me to do more of what I wanted to do and give me time to do things for me. I had just gotten my real estate license and was looking into different firms to sign with. I wanted to write this book (something I had been putting off for way too long), and most importantly, I really wanted to take the time to enjoy my life.

28

MORNING ROUTINES

For the longest time, I always started my day with an interesting struggle—the struggle to be "perfect," "the best," "the most liked." My old morning routine was wake up, check my email, Facebook, Instagram, Timehop, and Snapchat, and have my cup of coffee. I think social media only furthered my struggle with the image of perfection. The need to be "seen" and "heard." But the funny thing is, I don't really think this is the *right* kind of seen and heard.

Sometimes I still fall into starting my day by checking social media on my phone; however, I have been able to move away from it. I am still concerned with thoughts like *How many likes did my last picture on Instagram get? Did I use the right filter to make sure the picture looks just right? Does it look* perfect? But I know that there really is no *perfect*—and perfect is boring. I love the fact that there is so much beauty in the imperfections and quirks of people and things. So why do I still let those thoughts into my head? I think it's because of the box we're put into and the way our society says we should look, act, and feel.

Finally, though, I've found a way to begin my morning that really puts me in a positive place to start my day. When I joined Jameson Sotheby's International Realty in Chicago as a real estate broker, I went through a training taught by my managing broker. Immediately after signing on with the company, I knew I had found my home. My managing broker, Jim, is a huge advocate for self-development as a tool to succeed in business. Although I had grown up around these ideas, I had never really put them into practice. So when I started Jim's class, I promised myself I would do everything he said and really begin this new venture the right way.

One of the major things we talked about was the importance of morning rituals: waking up early, doing self-development work, planning out your day, meditating, and focusing on success. Sounds easy, right? Well, it took me a good month or two to really put it into motion.

I have always been an early riser, so the waking up early part wasn't hard for me. It was what I did in those early hours that needed to change. Typically, I wake up at 4:30 a.m. and begin my day. Now, instead of playing on my phone and using social media while I'm still in bed, I spend time watching motivational TED Talks or YouTube videos of motivational speakers or self-development gurus whom I trust and find inspiring. I make a list of the important things I need to get done for the day, and I spend some time visualizing my goals and what I want to get out of the hours ahead. It helps me focus the day; it helps me settle into my true self before getting involved with others.

I have come to see that the more grounded I am before starting my day, the less likely I am to doubt myself and let people get into my head. I have a better sense of self, and my confidence is so much greater than it was before. These days it is more difficult for images to affect me and throw me off track.

29

Being "Good"

I have always been a very giving and caring person, sometimes to a fault. I am constantly thinking about what I can do to make other people happy or to make them feel special. I guess I had never really thought much about that until I turned thirty.

I think my need and want to make everyone happy comes from a true, honest desire to help others and spread love, happiness, and joy—but I think there is also a little bit that stems from wanting to be "good," to be "perfect." This was a hard realization for me to come to. It's a trait that is hidden in my innate personality, and it took me a long time and a lot of therapy to be able to separate out my motivations.

When people are going through a hard time, I usually send them flowers or cards or something. Growing up, I had always noticed my mom doing it, so it just became second nature to me—much like writing hand-written thank-you notes. It's just something you do. But in my personal life I noticed a pattern of doing things because I thought it was what the other person wanted. I took a couple of jobs because I had a hard time saying no. I agreed with boyfriends because I didn't want to start an argument. I said yes to going out with people or participating in things that I really had no interest in.

Part of this is the normal course of life, and for those who don't have a problem taking into account what's best for them, it probably doesn't make sense. I think I really made the choice at the end of 2015 to make 2016 "my year." I don't typically make resolutions because, to me, they feel like a setup. So instead, I just kept saying, "2016 is going to be my year." In my mind, that meant doing things that made me happy and that I knew deep down I truly wanted to do. It meant being 100 percent okay saying no to people and saying yes to myself.

I have noticed a *huge* shift in my energy, outlook, and happiness. I have been more successful in every aspect of my life—professionally, romantically, and in my relationships with my family and myself. Suddenly, things don't feel like so much *work*. It all feels very positive, and I look forward to waking up in the morning and seeing what another day has in store. I feel healthier, look healthier, and have a ton more energy.

30

POWERFUL BEYOND MEASURE

*Our deepest fear is not that we are
inadequate. Our deepest fear is that we
are powerful beyond measure. It is our
light, not our darkness that most fright-
ens us. We ask ourselves who am I to be
brilliant, gorgeous, talented, fabulous?
Actually, who are you not to be? You are
a child of God. You playing small does
not serve the world. There is nothing
enlightened about shrinking so that other
people won't feel insecure around you. We
are all meant to shine, as children do. We
were born to make manifest the glory of
God that is within us. It is not just in
some of us; it is in everyone. And as we
let our own light shine, we unconsciously
give other people permission to do the*

same. As we are liberated from our own
fear, our presence automatically liberates
others.

—*Marianne Williamson*

This quote has deeply impacted my life. If I were talking to Oprah, I would say this was my "aha moment."

It had been some time since the accident, and I was talking to my dad about life, about how I knew I was meant to do something greater, and that was why I had survived. There was a lot of work still unfinished. My dad handed me a laminated card and when I flipped it over I found the Williamson quote. I read it, and I felt a sense of pride, accomplishment, responsibility, and purpose. I was proud of myself for never giving up, for refusing to choose the victim route, and for making it to where I was in life.

I still feel that way. I have a sense of accomplishment in terms of who I am and what I have achieved. I have gone through a lot. I have been through many ups and downs, and I am still standing. I am a fighter and I am very resilient, and I take a lot of pride in those two things. Every time I read this quote (and I read it on a daily basis), I continue to feel a sense of responsibility and purpose. As a human being and a woman, I feel it is my duty to inspire others, to celebrate their successes, and to lead by example.

The last two sentences of Marianne Williamson's quote really speak to me: *"And as we let our own light shine, we unconsciously give other people permission to do the same. As we are liberated from our own fear, our presence automatically liberates others."* When I think about this and take into account what I know about the power of intention and thought, it really hits me how powerful it is. It is rare to find someone who is truly rooting for you to succeed, someone who is always in your corner.

I am lucky to have had many people who have constantly cheered me on, but as I continue to go out into the world and meet others, I realize not everyone has had that luxury. So I've taken it upon myself to be this person for my friends. I am genuinely thrilled when they succeed and things are going well in their lives.

I am continuously learning to let my own light shine. It is a struggle. There are days where I still feel like I "play small" to make others feel more comfortable; but now, those days are few and far between. The place I found myself doing this most was in my romantic relationships. I felt the need to quiet myself or hide my true thoughts or feelings in order to avoid conflict or confrontation. I no longer feel this way, and if I catch myself slipping into this old pattern, I take a deep breath, remember this quote, and speak my truth.

Once I started to focus my energy on letting my own light shine and being the biggest cheerleader for my friends and family, I noticed a shift. My life is filled with happiness and love. I have been presented with an influx of opportunities because I am no longer squashing my "bigness" and my "light." Before I learned this lesson, I would never have sat down and taken the time to write this book. I always knew I had some ideas, and that the accident was a story I could tell, but beyond that I never felt like I had anything of value to share. That was me *not* letting my light shine, trying to dull it, making excuses, and not celebrating my *bigness*.

Thoughts on Theater

31

Speak Your Truth

The stage has always been the place where I felt most comfortable. It's the place where there are absolutely no consequences, the only place where you have the liberty and ability to do whatever you want and can then walk offstage and leave it all behind. That's part of why I have loved performing, why I was so drawn to the stage and theater. I could speak my truth and not worry about the outcome. I approached acting this way, bringing myself to the character and finding the little part in me that was also in the character. Then all my actions were based in truth. It made me feel, think, act, and respond in the most honest way. This is also why I became so good at being "good," at not making waves, not creating problems, and being a people pleaser. In real life, there are consequences. Conflict doesn't just go away and your words don't just disappear when you leave the room.

A quote by Steppenwolf Theatre Ensemble member Amy Morton has really inspired me both onstage and off:

> When you are onstage, you have license to do what everyone in the audience has wanted to do five thousand times, whether it is kill, love, hate, fuck, or fly. Only you get to do it with no consequences. Do it all the way. Never let your audience live vicariously through you in a mediocre way.

When I spent time onstage, in a land of no consequences, I could kill, love, and scream at someone with no real-world ramifications. I got to release all these actual emotions, but the minute I came out from behind those lights, that person fell off and my life was back to normal.

While this quote applies 100 percent to the stage (obviously, I don't go around every day killing, hating, fucking, or flying), it also directly relates to how I want to live my life and stand in my power. I am slowly learning to do conflict in a real way. Whether it's loving or fighting, you need to do everything 100 percent. It not only creates deeper relationships, but it is what makes you who you are. It makes people interesting and makes them stand out. For the longest time, I was convinced my voice didn't matter. My ideas weren't as good as others'.

I was just another person in a crowd. Once I realized that I had the ability, the right, and the responsibility to be who I was, and to be that person 100 percent, that's when I knew I was making a difference, connecting on a deeper level, and solidifying relationships that would last a lifetime.

32

STAYING OUTSIDE THE BOX

I always felt like I was put into a box, a box with only room enough for what society told me I should be and what I should do. I am a white woman who grew up on the North Shore of Chicago and that meant I should act a certain way, look a certain way, be a certain person, wear certain clothes, and do a certain thing. I should date a certain guy, have a certain job, and get paid a certain amount of money. This box was something I always accepted as my norm, something I never fought until I found Black Box Acting School. The Black Box method trains actors to work consistently from the most honest and brave place possible and to always be present, free, and open onstage. One of the key things they teach is to trust that you are enough. As I continued through all of their studio classes, B1 through B4, I gained more confidence in my acting, in my voice, and in myself. Is it a coincidence that the word *box* is in the name of the school? It was Black Box that shattered my need to fit into the box of someone I was not. It was where I was fully able to step into my power and into the most authentic version of who I am.

In September 2014, I decided to get a tattoo with Jessica, the friend I went with to see James Van Praagh. We had been talking about it for months and we had finally decided on our designs. Our friend Sarah came with us for moral support.

Jessica had recently lost her father, and I had found a more powerful self—we both wanted to mark the occasions. She got the quote "Our Father Who Art in Heaven" in white ink on her forearm, and I got a black box on my ribcage. I was terrified and extremely excited. I had heard the ribcage is the most sensitive area and it kills to get a tattoo there, but I wanted to have it in a place that wasn't very visible. I mean, I love showing off my tattoo and you can see it when I wear certain tops, dresses, and bathing suits, but I really wanted it to be just for me, something that I knew was there and that would keep me on the right path.

We walked into the tattoo parlor and checked in. We had previously sent our designs in, and they were prepared when we got there. Of course, my tattoo artist was ready first and asked, "Who has the square?" My friends were dying laughing.

I said, "That would be me," and went to the back and lay on the table. He asked me what the tattoo meant to me and why I was getting it. I explained, "It is a reminder

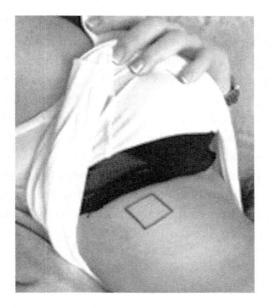

My box tattoo.

of who I am and who I don't want to be. I have learned so much about myself over the past seven years, and I couldn't think of any one thing that would signify my journey until I went through this acting school. Their motto is 'Work hard and be fearless,' and as much as I applied it to my acting, I applied it to my everyday life as well. It's a way for me to remind myself to never get trapped in the box society tries to put me in, a reminder to always speak my truth and to stand in my power, even when it scares me."

I went on to explain the freedom I felt when I finally realized who I was instead of who society and others wanted me to be. It felt as if I'd broken free from chains, like my life could finally begin. I had always felt like something was holding me back, holding me down, and stopping me from doing what I wanted to do. When I realized it was *me* who was holding me back, things shifted. *I finally got out of my own way.* I stopped listening to what others wanted and started paying attention to what I wanted. It was the most powerful thing I could have realized.

I owe this to Black Box, my friends and family, and, most importantly, to myself. For doing the real work, struggling through the tough times, and always finding a way to make it out alive.

33

CUPID AND PSYCHE

To a performer, one of the scariest things that can happen is memory loss. Everything depends on memory: your lines, simple tasks, and even navigating your day.

In 2008, a year after the accident, I decided it was time to get my ass back in the saddle and return to the stage. I was terrified. I was having a lot of difficulty remembering how to do daily tasks; how on earth was I supposed to remember the copious amounts of blocking, lines, and homework that are essential to a play? I auditioned anyway. It was for a play called *Cupid and Psyche,* which was being performed at our local community college and directed by a good friend of mine. I showed up, read my scenes, and landed the lead role of Psyche. I was excited and terrified, and yes, it was time to work my ass off.

Memorizing was always the easiest part for me. I would typically spend a couple of hours a day and within a few weeks, I would know the show from start to finish. That wasn't quite the case with this performance. Nevertheless, my therapists were all very excited that I was doing the show and getting back into a normal routine. They were happy I would be using my brain for something I loved and exercising it outside of our speech and occupational therapy sessions.

Memorizing my part took countless hours, tears, stress, and anxiety. I recruited the help of family and friends to run lines with me day and night. I loaded up on lots of good antioxidants and omega-3s to aid my memory. It was super frustrating and a lot of work, but extremely rewarding.

The feeling I got during rehearsals was one I felt deep down inside my core. It was such a tidal wave of power and truth, knowing that I belonged on this stage. I remember thinking, *I am meant to do this.* Opening night I was so nervous, I wanted to throw up. I still felt all the same fears, excitement, and energy I had felt during shows before the accident, but I also had a sense of the unknown living inside me: *What if my mind goes blank?* It had happened countless times during my recovery and was always really difficult to come back from. It took me out of the moment, and it wasn't something that I could recover from without everyone noticing.

I came up with a prayer—nine years later—that I was still saying before every performance. "Please keep me safe on stage. Keep me out of my head and with my scene partner. Please let me into the audience's heart and let whomever needs to hear this story receive the message they need. Please let me have fun and enjoy every moment I am out there. David, this is for you." That night was the first night I dedicated my performance to David, and now, countless performances later, I still do.

I remember my parents beaming with pride on opening night. Friends and family came from far and wide to see me do what I love. The show sold out for pretty much the whole run. I am so blessed to have the incredible support system I have.

The biggest takeaway from this show was "I can do it." Where there had once been an incredible amount of doubt, fear, and anxiety, there was now a sense of accomplishment, pride, and excitement to do the next show. Conquering such a huge fear (one that was pretty much made clear to me in the hospital: not to expect too much too quickly) gave me such a sense of power.

I don't think the director, Tony, knows exactly what that show meant to me or how much that experience changed my life and set me back onto my path. When I felt like giving up, he was there to encourage me, granting me breaks when I needed them and letting me take a minute to freak out before moving forward. It is one of the productions I hold near and dear to my heart and will cherish forever.

34

BLACK BOX ACTING STUDIO AND THE ACADEMY

I n February 2012 during rehearsals for our first show, *The Sweetest Swing in Baseball,* our director, Audrey, told us that Black Box was going to make a huge announcement the next day—something big and exciting was about to happen.

I remember the day the ACADEMY, Black Box Acting's most intensive training program, was announced. The conservatory runs for a hundred days and trains actors to "Work Hard and Be Fearless." It was a nine-month program, an immersion in Meisner acting technique, Viewpoints, Text Analysis, Classics, and TV/Film with individualized instruction led by the Black Box ACADEMY instructors. Admission was based on an application and audition, and there would be a final graduation showcase in front of leading industry professionals in Chicago. When I heard about this program, I knew I had to apply. This was exactly what I needed to do for my process as an actor and for myself. I had always felt a little cheated that I didn't get to finish my acting program at LMU because of my accident, and I knew this was the right experience for me now.

I filled out the application and wrote my personal statement as to why I wanted to study at the ACADEMY:

The number one reason why I want to study at the ACADEMY is because I am absolutely terrified of studying at the ACADEMY. The things that I fear the most are usually the things I should immerse myself in, to tap into the places of fear that hold me back. The intensity and fear are essential for me to be able to progress as an actor, as it is my barometer for detecting authentic, passionate, and fundamental training that will help release the emotional bindings that hold me back in my work.

This feeling led me to my first Black Box class that began in October of 2010. From the first day, I knew I had found an incredible training opportunity. I remember getting into the car when my sister picked me up and telling her that the class was one of the most intense and fruitful emotional workouts I had been through. My "acting muscles" were sore, burning, and it was a liberating feeling. I knew I had found a home where I could stretch and grow as an actor. Black Box has completely changed the way I act, and I want more.

Black Box's method of teaching awakens the core of my being and pushes me to acknowledge the deepest truths of the world, others, and myself. I believe great acting cannot exist in the absence of this exploration. Black Box's unique and fierce commitment to developing the fearless actor will help deepen my skills and further my process as an actor in ways I believe no other conservatory would. I look forward to the opportunity to take the fundamental skills that I have learned in my B1–B4 and Audition classes and enhance my ability to be open, honest, present, and connected at all times onstage.

I hope to bring a strong sense of commitment to the program, with a sincere dedication and unrelenting commitment to developing my skills as an actor. A personal goal for this upcoming year is to allow and trust that my homework resides within me, but simultaneously let go and commit to the ride with my partner. I plan to seize every opportunity to learn, grow, and challenge myself as an actor and to trust an authentic expression of who I am.

It was an incredible nine-month process. It wasn't always easy—in fact, most of the time it was extremely difficult and I left class cursing my decision to do it. But then I began to feel as if I was on the brink of a breakthrough in finding my true voice as an artist. I made incredible friends in those nine months, many of whom

I am still extremely close with today. I laughed a lot, cried a lot, and pushed myself harder than I ever thought was possible. A ton of key points in my training were "breakthrough moments" for me, and I remember them happening like it was yesterday. One of the moments I am most proud of was during what was called "Choose Your Own Adventure Week."

We received our weekly homework email on a Friday, which said we were being given the freedom to do whatever we wanted to do for the next week. We were to think of one thing we'd always wanted to do but maybe never had the courage to try. We knew we would never find a safer space or a better group of people to support us. So over the weekend I did some major soul searching and tried to figure out what I wanted that next week to be for me. We could bring anything we wanted into class—stand-up comedy, sketch comedy, dance performance, musical theater pieces, videos. It only took me a day to figure out what I wanted to do. The one thing that would scare me the most would be sharing my accident story. I was excited and terrified to bring my *Ten Hours* piece to class on Monday and share it with everyone.

Over the course of the next few days, our instructor for the week, Laura, and I worked one on one to get the piece to where I'd feel uncomfortably comfortable sharing it with the group. Laura was my biggest cheerleader that week and I never could have gotten through it without her. I was so emotionally connected to the piece that the thought of sharing it felt like I would be standing completely naked in the room. I didn't share my work during the rehearsals for the show; Laura and I decided it would be better to save it for the performance. I had rehearsed it enough times with her privately that I felt like I could execute it without a "dress rehearsal."

In true Black Box form, they threw a curveball at us and told us they were opening our "Talent Show" up to the public and we could invite whomever we wanted. My family wasn't able to make it, but I invited two close friends whom I love and trust tremendously.

Why did I want to do this? As a Black Box artist you are taught from day one to always bring yourself to the table. I couldn't think of anything that was more honest and true to me than this story. Living through the accident and struggling through my recovery has changed my outlook on life. This story was my truth about what happened in those ten hours when I was unconscious on the side of the road. By sharing this piece, I was taking the next steps in sharing my truths. In the moment, the idea of showing that part of myself to the audience made me feel incredibly vulnerable yet empowered. It solidified my voice to me. It was one of the best decisions I made during my nine months at the ACADEMY.

35

Baggage

At the start of my post-accident journey, I had brought some baggage with me. My suitcase was packed with five things that were completely weighing me down: the need for constant validation, a sense of self-doubt, the feeling of being wronged, the need to apologize for things I didn't need to apologize for, and my "good girl" syndrome. Over time, I learned to unpack my suitcase and get rid of these things that I had been carrying around for my entire life. In the ten years since the accident, I have worked incredibly hard to learn the lessons that I have, and I am happy to say that I've gotten rid of the old contents of my suitcase. It's funny how life puts you in situations to help you gain the wisdom you need most. By the end of my ACADEMY journey, I had noticed that the unpacking and repacking of my bags mirrored my life, both onstage and off.

Looking back, I am amazed by my ability and my intention. Lying in the hospital bed, I decided that my life wasn't going to be the same as it was before the accident, that I was going to take the time to focus on me, the person I knew I truly was and who I wanted to be. By really looking at myself from the outside, by going through all that I did, and by making the effort to invest in me and my wants and needs, I have learned to live and work in a more fearless and brave way. I speak before I have a chance to let others cloud my voice, I jump when I know there may be nothing there to catch me, and I allow myself to follow my impulses.

I don't believe in coincidences, and I follow the firm belief that everything happens for a reason. One reason for that is because while I was learning these powerful tools in the ACADEMY, I was implementing them in my nonactor world. I had learned to truly love, own, and be proud of my entire self. That meant all of me, all of my crazy, my goofy-ness, and my unrealistic fears, the heartbreak, wants, needs, and desires, the scary, vulnerable, quirky, and gross parts—I love them all and I now *want* people to see them, because they make me who I am. They make me unique. They make me *beautiful*. Normal and perfect are boring. So my new suitcase holds my firm belief that I am enough, my ability to know and stand 100 percent behind my voice and my truth, and the fact that my power can never be taken away from me.

That first year and every year since the accident,

October 23 feels like my real birthday. It is the day I celebrate who I am and who I choose to be. I know things could have gone entirely differently for me post-accident. I could have gotten stuck in the drama and chosen to be the victim. I could have stayed depressed and refused to see the comedy in the situation. A lot could have been different. I have run those could haves, should haves, and would haves and to this day, I am so proud of what I chose. *I chose to live.* I made a conscious choice in 2007 and every day since to live my life to the fullest and with integrity. I don't sweat the small stuff. I eat healthy. I exercise. I talk to my parents every day. I call my siblings. I make sure the people I love know I love them. *I thank God every day for what happened to me.*

Yes, you read that correctly. People always say to me, "I am so sorry this happened to you." "I wish you never had to go through this." Now, don't get me wrong, I would never wish for it to happen to me again, but I am grateful for the experience. Ten years later, I can say I am really happy it happened. I was stuck in a life I had created for myself that was full of drama, angst, self-pity, and self-hate. The accident washed almost all of those things away. Sure, they come back from time to time (I am still a normal person and of course have self-doubt) but I do not let them control the way I act and what I think about myself. I am a stronger, wiser, happier person because of what I went through. I learned not to take things for granted. I learned to enjoy life. I learned to love deeply. I have been changed. The accident propelled me to look at myself and make sure I was on the path I wanted to be on. It made me question some of my past choices and make the conscious decision to leave this world a better place.

When the accident happened, it unconsciously broke any sort of pattern I had previously put in place for myself. It was as if my energy field and my psyche shattered along with the bones in my body. I was pretty much an infant again and had to rebuild the person I knew I wanted to be.

How cool is that? How many people get to say they have had a chance to completely start over? It wasn't easy and it wasn't always fun, but I know it was worth it.

Afterword

There have been many times in my life when I thought I would never get out of my slump, when I didn't know how I would get beyond my current state of feeling or thinking. It is a really tough place to be in. It's a challenging thing to feel depressed and depleted yet still have to face a day of work, friends, and personal life. It can be a real struggle sometimes. My lessons didn't all come overnight. It wasn't like I said to myself post-accident, "Hey, so now you're going to be different," and all my doubts, fears, and struggles went away. No, it took a lot of hard work, therapy, tears, heartbreak, and soul searching, but it was worth every single step. And, yes, occasionally I still slip back into old patterns and routines. Sometimes I still feel down, depressed, or stuck, but when I do, I try to remember a couple of things:

As my mom told me on my thirtieth birthday, "Feel the Feelings!" Don't ignore them. Ignoring the feelings will only make things worse. It's like telling your body and mind that they're wrong, that they don't know anything, when really they're the smartest, most reliable things you have. Your body knows things before your brain does. The tension you carry around in your body, the headaches, and even the happiness and lightness—they are all signs. They tell you things. So listen to them and try to figure out the source.

Do things that feed your soul. One practice I have adopted is to do things that feed me, even the little things. That means most mornings I start my day by reading quotes that are personally significant to me or by watching videos I like, such as Brené Brown's TED Talks or speeches by inspirational leaders. I read self-development books, sometimes a chapter in the morning or at night. I meditate and visualize what I want.

Simple pleasures. This means doing something simple that makes you smile. For me, it can be going to get a manicure or pedicure or heading to my favorite spot in my house. It can mean taking a walk or fitting in a workout. I love to stroll around Chicago and look at the beautiful architecture, buildings, and water. By the time I get back home I've usually worked through whatever it was that was getting me down. For me, one of the worst things I can do is sit at home and think. It's when I start to dwell that I get myself in trouble. I send myself down a hole and it's hard to get back out.

▲ ▼ ▲

One of the most challenging things for me has been to learn how to navigate the world of dating while remaining true to myself. Dating can be both exciting and terrifying, and the fear of getting hurt may never leave. Date anyway. Put yourself out there. The only way to know what you want in a relationship is to learn from your previous ones. The past teaches you what you want and don't want. It helps you see more clearly who you are, both in relationships and alone. You clearly learn what is significant to you and what is not. Never settle for less than what's on your "important list."

While I am the first one to know how incredibly hard breakups can be, I have also learned how valuable they are. Every single time I broke up with a guy, my mom said, "Well, honey, I know you're hurting, but maybe it's for the best. You don't want to be with someone who doesn't value and respect who you are. You have so much to offer and so much love to give. You want to be with someone who sees that and can never give it up."

I have heard this speech so many times that I could pretty much recite it word for word. In the moment, though, it was always extremely hard for me to take that wisdom in, and oftentimes I felt like no one would ever come along to show me why things hadn't worked out yet. Ultimately, though, a few months would go by and I would realize my mom was right. Those months weren't always fun, but I learned a lot about who I was as an individual and who I was in a relationship.

The biggest and most important lesson I have learned from dating is how to stay in my power and in my truth. Every relationship has helped me learn the importance of saying what's on my mind, because that is what *men* actually want. *Boys* may not want that—*boys* may want you to stay small so they're always the ones in control. But a real *man* will always want you to speak your truth, stand in your power, and be you.

So while some may criticize me for the number of relationships I have had, or call me "boy crazy" for my willingness to go on dating sites, or "too picky" in my wait for the right guy, I simply call it refusing to settle and doing research—research to find out what is important to me. While there have been many times when I was willing to shut myself down for a guy, I now know why none of those relationships worked and how lucky I am that I never settled.

In the spring of 2016 I decided I was going to go on two more dates through Match.com and then give it a break. I was getting overwhelmed by the site and disappointed by the guys I was meeting on it. So I told myself, "Okay, just go on these last two dates and then get off Match for a while." And that's what I did. The first guy was really gross—he reminded me of Leonardo DiCaprio's character in *The Wolf of Wall Street*, sadly not because of his looks but because of the way he threw his money around. Everything came back to how much money he had, what kind of car he owned, the places he shopped. I couldn't get out of there fast enough. I

RENEW and GET A FREE GIFT!

As a Preferred Member who appreciates the Smithsonian, you deserve this special renewal discount.

Renew your Smithsonian Membership today for just $12.00 — and get a FREE membership to give as a gift to a friend or family member. That's a <u>savings of $66.00</u> on 2 memberships, including your own.

Lock in your Preferred Member Savings

Simply complete and return the enclosed voucher by the deadline to claim your FREE Gift Membership.

THIS OFFER IS NOT TRANSFERABLE.

Smithsonian

went home defeated and not necessarily too optimistic about my next date.

I met Brian on St. Paddy's Day, on a rooftop in Chicago. We had drinks overlooking Millennium Park and the conversation flowed—it was an amazing time. We were both a little hungry so we continued the date and grabbed a bite to eat, followed by a game of oversized Jenga at a pub right by my house. He walked me home, kissed me goodnight (I rarely kiss on the first date), and asked when he could see me again. We made plans to get together later that week before I went out of town with my family for Easter.

Little did I know I had just gone on my last first date. Brian is everything I had been looking for. He is a *man* who is so authentic, so full of integrity, has a heart of gold, and would do anything for those he loves. He is a family man. He values the little things and doesn't take life too seriously. He knows how to have important conversations when we need to, but he is also somebody I can just goof around with and spend the day laughing with. Most importantly, he is someone I can be myself with—my authentic, vulnerable, dorky, weird, fun, caring, loving, and powerful self. He values my thoughts, my opinions, and my true voice. When I am with him, I can let my guard down. I love him dearly and trust him completely.

I know there are no accidents in the universe. As frustrating, heartbreaking, and exhausting as it was to date those *boys* who always broke my heart and didn't value me, respect me, or make me a priority, I know I couldn't have learned the truth about who I am, who I want to be, and who I want to be with any other way. I am so happy Brian didn't come into my life until after I turned thirty and had absorbed all these lessons. It has allowed me to let him in fully and let him see who I really am.

▲　▼　▲

I hope you have found this book helpful and there are some takeaways for you. I hope you can see that there is limitless power in going after what you want. Nobody can ever take away your determination and drive. There is such a force that ignites when you decide to put action behind your career, your relationships, and yourself. When you choose to be who you want to be and to live a life in integrity, staying away from the victim mentality, things seem to fall into place. Don't ever settle.

Remember: you set and create your own parameters; nobody has the power to tell you who you should or shouldn't be. It is your life, your rules, and your choice to break free from what others expect of you. And perhaps the most important lesson I hope you take away from this book is that *you* are beautiful, just the way you are. You do not need to change for anybody. You do not need to gain or lose weight, change your hair color, wear or not wear makeup. You, my darling, are gorgeous just the way you are.

Acknowledgments

I want to thank my mom and dad for always supporting me, encouraging me, and pushing me to be the best I can be. Cristina, Jenna, and Joe for being the best siblings a girl could ask for and for always having my back. Veronica and Auntie Jo, you are like my second moms; I wouldn't be who I am without you both in my life. To my nana and the rest of my extended family—thank you for your love. To Brian, for showing me what true love is, making me laugh every day, and for allowing me to be my true self and supporting me in every way. To all my friends, thank you for standing by my side in the good times and the bad. To all those I worked with at KN Literary Arts—Rebecca, Wendy, Chandika, Melissa, and Sheridan—this book would not have been possible without all your help, guidance, support, and hard work. Wini, thank you for being such a grounding force and voice in my life, helping me navigate my way through all the ups and downs, and celebrating all my successes and failures with me. To Jon Sweeney, Julie Walker, Jenniffer Weigel, and Dr. Therese Rowley, thank you for opening my eyes to the spiritual world and helping me

Acknowledgments

heal by connecting the dots for me. To all my doctors, nurses, and the staff at The Rehabilitation Insitute of Chicago—thank you for your care and your help in getting me back to health. And to my guardian angels in Heaven—Jackie Walker, Roxanne Malo, and Nana Nana—I know you have been with me every step of the way and I love you.

Further Resources

Jon Sweeney

Jon is an internationally known directed distant intentionality healer, founder of Co-Creative Coherence Therapy, and an ordained interfaith minister. He is a teacher, author, lecturer, musician, and artist. For more than a decade, he has served as a healing partner with individuals across the globe to heal the body and help the spirit soar using the Coherence Therapy method and quantum consciousness. www.spiritwords.com.

Julie Walker

Julie serves as a medical intuitive from her home base of Wilmette, Illinois. Over the years she has worked with peoples from all over the globe in the healing arts. For almost a decade she lived in Swaziland and South Africa with her family, where she worked with traditional healers from various regions. While in Swaziland, she began to explore and develop models of evolution related to healing and the sciences based on observations of universal patterns of change. Currently, she is developing applications and materials for the Oneness

Model related to evolution. She also gives workshops on Changes and Choices, *The Oneness Model,* and *The Little Book of the Soul's Big Journey.* www.onenessmodel.com.

Black Box Acting

Black Box Acting is a school dedicated to training actors in how to "Work Hard and Be Fearless." Its three training programs are:

- The ACADEMY: A five-month intensive conservatory training
- The STUDIO: Part-time classes and workshops offered year round
- National Intensives: Boot camp–style Black Box training in cities across the country

All three programs teach the Black Box Method. This comprehensive and rigorous curriculum, based on Meisner and Viewpoints, trains actors to:

- Be in the moment and feel alive onstage
- Celebrate flaws and gifts equally
- Live fully under imagined circumstances
- Own text with honesty and integrity
- Follow physical impulses
- Work from an honest, brave, and present place … consistently

Blackboxacting.com.

Jenniffer Weigel

Jen is an award-winning broadcast journalist from Chicago who started in radio and eventually moved to television, where she was a reporter and news anchor.

She won an Emmy for her on-camera reporting for CBS. After her father (broadcaster and journalist Tim Weigel) died of a brain tumor in 2001, she decided life was too short to shiver on an overpass, reporting, "It's cold outside. Back to you." She started her own production company and hosted the Emmy-nominated food and wine show called *Taste* for NBC in Chicago. She has written three books: *Stay Tuned, I'm Spiritual, Dammit!* and *This Isn't the Life I Ordered.*

Jen worked with the *Chicago Tribune* from 2010 to 2015 as a columnist ("Lessons for Life") and a reporter (lifestyles, travel, food, and the Remarkable Woman column). She now hosts *Conversations with Weigel: A Series Exploring Spiritual Enlightenment* at the Wilmette Theatre once a month, interviewing authors and gurus from across the country. Her podcast, *I'm Spiritual, Dammit!*, is one of the most popular podcasts for WGN-plus. www.jenweigel.com.

Therese Rowley, PhD

Therese Rowley, PhD, is passionate about supporting global leaders to operate in full power, high energy, and clear focus that encourages their meaningful engagement in business and in life. Through her company, Accelerated Alignment, Dr. Rowley is a trusted advisor to CEOs and C-Suite executives as they make high-impact business decisions, and she supports them through the challenges of personal and organizational transformation. As a consultant, educator, speaker, author, and skilled intuitive, she uses her intuitive ability to reveal hidden data, resulting in powerful, precise, and accelerated business decisions. She has provided thousands of intuitive readings, and she sees intuitive intelligence as an essential literacy for twenty-first century leaders.

Therese's Intuitive Sessions offer immediate and powerful breakthroughs when you feel stuck, overwhelmed, confused, or indecisive. They provide profound insight that works at the soul level to release emotional, psychological, and spiritual blocks that are underpinning your current or persistent challenge. Specifically, they offer information and healing so you can:

- Reclaim or unleash your power during times of significant change
- Receive crystal clarity for decisions that mean the most to you
- Find peace because you understand why things happened as they did
- Gain alignment as you feel released from fear and fear-based beliefs
- Gain clarity about relationships—those you want, those you don't want, and those with ones who have passed over

http://thereserowley.com.

Step Up Chicago Playwrights (formerly Step Up Productions)

Step Up Chicago Playwrights is a nonprofit center for new play development. It develops original plays about the diverse communities of Chicago, leads playwriting workshops, and provides developmental assistance for small theaters in Chicago. Through commissions and workshops, it fosters new Chicago plays and playwrights, ultimately promoting them to the American theater community.

Step Up Chicago Playwrights' mission is to help theater look and sound more like Chicago—*all* of Chicago—by supporting communities who want their stories told and the playwrights who are willing to step up and tell them. Its plays represent untold stories about homelessness, substance abuse, mental or physical disabilities, national origin, sexual orientation, gender identity, race, color, veteran status, religion, and more. As a result of its work, it hopes to inspire people to examine their own lives, truths, and actions—maybe someone will volunteer somewhere or do something they have always wanted to do after hearing someone else's story on stage. http://www.stepupchicagoplaywrights.com.

Dana Marie—Singer-Songwriter

Born and raised in Chicago, emerging country singer-songwriter Dana Marie moved to Nashville in January 2016. Within the past year, she has had the honor of opening up for country artists such as Jana Kramer and Dallas Smith. Now, together with her band, she performs on stages on the legendary Broadway strip in downtown Nashville. Her musical influences include Miranda Lambert, Kacey Musgraves, Bob Marley, Colbie Caillat, and Zac Brown Band, among many others. She draws inspiration from all types of music, but country music just "feels like home."

Besides her obvious love for music, Dana loves spending time outdoors. She loves the simple things—summer nights, handwritten lyrics, guys who can two-step, quality time with family and friends, baseball games, live music, vanilla cupcakes, puppies, and hugs that linger just a moment longer than usual.

Dana uses her platform as a musician to empower young women and inspire them to shine. She openly shares her story of struggling with Crohn's Disease and living with an ileostomy in order to show others that we are only limited by our own beliefs. Dana believes that there always is a silver lining; we just have to be willing to find it. She's on a mission to inspire others to follow their hearts—because when you shine, you give others permission to do the same. http://danamarieband.com.

Riverside Puppies

Riverside Puppies takes pride in raising healthy and well-socialized puppies. All of its pets are registered and in perfect health. It is located in Missouri's Ozark Hills overlooking the Gasconade River. Its adult dogs are not just breeding animals; they are cherished pets and allowed to run and play on their farm. Riverside Puppies has 250 acres of rolling hills—lots of room for family and pets. Its horses and cattle graze on green grass, with plenty of room to run. http://www.riversidepuppies.biz.

About the Author

Elizabeth Antonucci is the founding director of the nonprofit company Step Up Chicago Playwrights and is on its advisory board. Through her charitable and nonprofit work and this book, she aims to share her experiences, promote acceptance and self-love, and help others find their authentic voice. Elizabeth lives in Clovis, California, with her fiancé, Brian, and is a volunteer at Big Brothers Big Sisters of Central California.

CPSIA information can be obtained
at www.ICGtesting.com
Printed in the USA
BVOW10s2142020817

491000BV00012B/371/P

9 780998 910406